A STUDY GUIDE TO
THE CHINESE: ADAPTING THE PAST,
BUILDING THE FUTURE

by
Thomas M. Buoye

**with the assistance of
Gail Tirana**

Made possible by a grant from
General Electric

The University of Michigan
Center for Chinese Studies
Ann Arbor

1986

ISBN 0–89264–072–3

Printed in the United States of America

CONTENTS

ACKNOWLEDGMENTS   v

NOTE TO THE STUDENT   vii

COURSE OUTLINE   x

UNITS OF STUDY

Part One: History and Geography
   Unit One: History   1
   Unit Two: Geographic and Ethnic Diversity   10
   Essay/Discussion Questions   16

Part Two: Politics
   Unit Three: Ideology and Organization   19
   Unit Four: The Individual and the State   27
   Essay/Discussion Questions   32

Part Three: Society
   Unit Five: The Chinese Family   37
   Unit Six: Creating a Broader Community   43
   Unit Seven: Cleavages and Social Conflicts   49
   Essay/Discussion Questions   55

Part Four: The Economy
   Unit Eight: Agriculture   61
   Unit Nine: Industry   66
   Unit Ten: Trade   72
   Essay/Discussion Questions   78

iv

Part Five: Culture
    Unit Eleven: Literature and the Arts   83
    Unit Twelve: Science and Technology   87
    Essay/Discussion Questions   92

Part Six: The Future
    Unit Thirteen: China's Prospects   97
    Essay/Discussion Question   102

APPENDICES

1. Maps and Other Aids   105
2. *Pinyin* Pronunciation Guide   107
3. *Pinyin*/Wade-Giles Conversion Chart   108

ACKNOWLEDGMENTS

Several people have contributed their time and talents to the production of this *Study Guide*. Jane Scheiber of NVC did the editing; her experience was invaluable in keeping the guide accessible to the lay reader. Gail Tirana, also of NVC, contributed to the editing and wrote the review and discussion questions. My good friend Diane Scherer of the Center of Chinese Studies proofed early drafts and prepared the camera-ready copy; her extensive knowledge of Chinese history contributed greatly to the finished product. James Hynes, the Center's editor, copyedited the guide and supervised its production. Finally, special thanks to Mi Qingliu.

Tom Buoye

NOTE TO THE STUDENT

This guide is intended to help both the general student of Chinese studies and the student enrolled for credit in the telecourse, *The Chinese: Adapting the Past, Building the Future.* The *Study Guide* is not meant to substitute for a critical reading and viewing of the course materials. Rather, it is intended to clarify issues and assist the student in integrating the diverse materials and opinions presented in the video and printed components of the course.

The course materials consist of the twelve fifty-minute video programs, "The Heart of the Dragon," which were broadcast over PBS for the first time in spring 1985; the companion book, *The Heart of the Dragon,* by Alasdair Clayre; the Reader, or anthology, of articles, poems, and documents entitled *The Chinese: Adapting the Past, Building the Future,* edited by Robert F. Dernberger, Kenneth J. DeWoskin, Steven M. Goldstein, Rhoads Murphey, and Martin K. Whyte; and this *Study Guide.* The *Study Guide* is divided into six parts, corresponding to the divisions of the Reader: (1) History and Geography; (2) Politics; (3) Society; (4) the Economy; (5) Culture; and (6) the Future.

Each part of the *Study Guide* begins with a general statement of the scope of that section of the course. The discussion is then broken down into units that correspond to the individual chapters of the Reader and the video programs. For each unit there is a listing of study components, followed by a list of learning objectives—some of the basic understandings of the issues that the course designers hope you will develop. This is followed by an overview that discusses the readings for each unit and relates them to one another and to the video, showing how together they present an integrated approach to the topic under consideration. Key concepts and definitions highlight some of the major ideas presented in the unit and explain terms that may be unfamiliar. Factual review questions enable you to test your own knowledge of the material. Finally, returning to a consideration of the broader, most comprehensive aims of the course, the *Study Guide* provides a set of essay/

discussion questions designed to test your ability to integrate facts and to use them in a discussion, as well as to serve as a review and stimulus to further thought about the issues.

Although each student will discover for himself or herself how best to use the course materials, we would suggest the following approach:

1. Glance over the learning objectives, overview, and key concepts for the appropriate section in the *Study Guide*. These will call attention to some of the more important points of the course and will help to focus your study.

2. View the video component, taking notes as necessary.

3. Read the corresponding section in the companion book, *The Heart of the Dragon*, which largely parallels and amplifies the video material.

4. Read the appropriate selections in the Reader.

5. Reread the overview and key concepts, considering them more thoroughly this time.

6. Proceed to the factual review questions, rereading the materials as necessary to answer them.

7. Turn back to the learning objectives. Have you met these goals?

8. Consider the essay/discussion questions. Suggested guidelines to answers are provided with each question, but there is, of course, no single "correct" answer.

9. Check the bibliographies in the Reader for suggestions for further reading on topics of interest.

We suggest that in studying and organizing these materials the student make full use of the chronological tables and maps that appear on the inside covers and in the opening pages of Clayre's book, *The Heart of the Dragon*.

The concepts and information provided in this course are complex; a complete understanding of a nation as large, varied, and old as China cannot be provided within the scope of a single course. Rather, it has been the purpose of the designers of this course to introduce a primarily Western audience to a civilization that is, in many ways, very different from their own and to begin to develop in that audience an understanding of the rich heritage that the Chinese bring with them as they face the problems of modernization in the last years of the twentieth century. We hope that this study guide will aid in this process.

Jane Scheiber

COURSE OUTLINE

PART ONE: HISTORY AND GEOGRAPHY

UNIT ONE: HISTORY

Video: "Remembering"
The Heart of the Dragon, by Alasdair Clayre: Chapter
One, "Remembering"
The Chinese: Chapter One, "History"

UNIT TWO: GEOGRAPHIC AND ETHNIC DIVERSITY

Video: "Eating"
The Heart of the Dragon, by Alasdair Clayre: Chapter
Five, "Eating"
The Chinese: Chapter Two, "Geographic and Ethnic
Diversity"

PART TWO: POLITICS

UNIT THREE: IDEOLOGY AND ORGANIZATION

Video: "Believing"
The Heart of the Dragon, by Alasdair Clayre: Chapter
Five, "Believing"
The Chinese: Chapter Three, "Ideology and Organization"

UNIT FOUR: THE INDIVIDUAL AND THE STATE

Video: "Correcting"
The Heart of the Dragon, by Alasdair Clayre: Chapter
Eight, "Correcting"
The Chinese: Chapter Four, "The Individual and the
State"

PART THREE: SOCIETY

UNIT FIVE: THE CHINESE FAMILY

Video: "Marrying"
The Heart of the Dragon, by Alasdair Clayre: Chapter
  Three, "Marrying"
The Chinese: Chapter Five, "The Chinese Family"

UNIT SIX: CREATING A BROADER COMMUNITY

Video: "Caring"
The Heart of the Dragon, by Alasdair Clayre: Chapter
  Four, "Mediating," pp. 91–104
The Chinese: Chapter Six, "Creating a Broader Com-
  munity"

UNIT SEVEN: CLEAVAGES AND SOCIAL CONFLICTS

Video: "Mediating"
The Heart of the Dragon, by Alasdair Clayre: Chapter
  Four, "Mediating," pp. 104–7
The Chinese: Chapter Seven, "Cleavages and Social Con-
  flicts"

PART FOUR: THE ECONOMY

UNIT EIGHT: AGRICULTURE

Video: "Living"
The Heart of the Dragon, by Alasdair Clayre: Chapter Six,
  "Living"
The Chinese: Chapter Eight, "Agriculture"

UNIT NINE: INDUSTRY

Video: "Working"
The Heart of the Dragon, by Alasdair Clayre: Chapter
  Seven, "Working"
The Chinese: Chapter Nine, "Industry"

UNIT TEN: TRADE

Video: "Trading"
The Heart of the Dragon, by Alasdair Clayre: Chapter
   Eleven, "Trading"
The Chinese: Chapter Ten, "Trade"

PART FIVE: CULTURE

UNIT ELEVEN: LITERATURE AND THE ARTS

Video: "Creating"
The Heart of the Dragon, by Alasdair Clayre: Chapter
   Ten, "Creating"
The Chinese: Chapter Eleven, "Literature and the Arts"

UNIT TWELVE: SCIENCE AND TECHNOLOGY

Video: "Understanding"
The Heart of the Dragon, by Alasdair Clayre: Chapter
   Nine, "Understanding"
The Chinese: Chapter Twelve, "Science and Technology"

PART SIX: THE FUTURE

UNIT THIRTEEN: CHINA'S PROSPECTS

The Chinese: Chapter Thirteen: "China's Prospects"

Part One
History and Geography

Part One introduces the historical and geographic factors that provide keys to understanding the China of today—and tomorrow. Highlighting some of the major developments in Chinese history from 2000 B.C. to the present, this section of the course focuses on the importance of the "Great Tradition" to the Chinese people today and on the political and cultural forces that have unified China despite the great variety of its regions and its peoples.

UNIT ONE: HISTORY

Study Components

Video: "Remembering"

The Heart of the Dragon, by Alasdair Clayre: Chapter One, "Remembering"

Readings from *The Chinese*: Introduction to Part One and Chapter One, "History"

1. "The Old Order," by John K. Fairbank

2. "Sung Society: Change Within Tradition," by E. A. Kracke, Jr.

3. "China's Response to the West," edited by Ssu-yu Teng and John K. Fairbank

4. "Modern China in Transition, 1900–50," by Mary C. Wright

Learning Objectives

To become acquainted with:

— a general outline of Chinese history

— Confucian ideology and its influence on Chinese culture and political and social institutions

— the transformation of traditional society and political institutions in the modern era

— Mao Zedong's role in modern Chinese politics

— the "Great Tradition" and the strength of historical consciousness in modern China

Overview

Chinese civilization has survived for over 4,000 years and no summary of Chinese history can adequately do justice to its richness and complexity. Nevertheless, Rhoads Murphey's introductory essay to Part One of *The Chinese* and the first chapter of *The Heart of the Dragon* by Alasdair Clayre combine to provide a succinct outline of the Chinese past. (See also pp. xi-xiii of *The Heart of the Dragon* for a chronological table of Chinese history.) The imperial system based on Confucian principles was established during the eastern Han dynasty (206 B.C.–220 A.D.) and it remained the basis of Chinese government until the Republican Revolution of 1911. Although China experienced periods of disorder and foreign domination, the imperial tradition and Chinese culture remained intact. For centuries Chinese culture dominated East Asia and influenced the cultures and political institutions of neighboring countries. As both writers point out, the Chinese are very "past conscious" and their history is a source of great pride.

As John Fairbank explains in "The Old Order," the ancient principles of Confucian government, which have been explicitly repudiated since 1949, are central to an understanding of China's history. In contemporary China, even though the principles of Marxism, Leninism, and Mao Zedong Thought have supplanted Confucianism, such notions as the belief in the perfectibility of individuals are evident in the modern emphasis on political education. The Confucian concept of the individual as perfectible and having an innate moral sense influenced the Confucian philosophy of government and, together with even older Chinese understandings of the relationship between humans and nature and the concept of rule by the "Mandate of Heaven," have influenced Chinese society, culture, and political organization. The values of Confucian ideology were embodied by the scholar-gentry class, which was the main source of government officials and hence instrumental in preserving the imperial system. Fairbank also illuminates very basic Chinese attitudes toward the role of the ruler in maintaining harmony between humankind and the rest of nature, government by moral example, hierarchical social order, centralized government, and the place of the individual in society. (Note that many of these attitudes are very different from those held by most Westerners.) These topics are discussed further in subsequent sections of the *Study Guide*, as they are relevant to various aspects of Chinese tradition.

E. A. Kracke's article examines the Song (Sung) dynasty, a period many historians consider an important turning point in Chinese history. Yet, as Kracke notes, it was a period of "change within tradition." The Song dynasty witnessed a shift in population from northern China to the agriculturally rich south. This shift in population stimulated an expansion of commerce and with it a burgeoning merchant class. The growth of urban areas and of a system of currency and credit also reached unprecedented levels, though China remained primarily an agrarian society. The imperial examination system became the predominant method for bureaucratic recruitment and many of the new recruits were from urban areas, probably from families who had acquired their wealth from commerce. Prior to the Song many officials came from aristocratic families whose wealth was based in landholding. Expanding the scope of bureaucratic recruitment also meant greater power for the emperor, since these new recruits owed their status solely to having passed the imperial examinations. Thus, as Kracke shows, although the foundations of the Chinese polity remained the same, significant changes occurred within the traditional order. Published in 1955, this essay is also important because it anticipated a trend among Western historians away from the notion of traditional China as a changeless society.

The Chinese concept of a hierarchical society and polity, which placed the emperor, as the "son of heaven," at the pinnacle of power, was physically represented in the architecture of the Forbidden City, as the video "Remembering" carefully traces. This concept of the unique status of the emperor and the Chinese empire was also extended to foreign relations. Prior to the nineteenth century, countries seeking diplomatic and commercial ties with China were required to accept the Chinese notion that they were tributary states of the Chinese empire. The documents translated by Fairbank and Ssu-yu Teng reveal the application of these Chinese attitudes toward the early intrusion of militant Western commercial powers and the growing perception of the threat these powers posed to China. The memorial of the Qianlong emperor to King George III of England displays the patronizing tone of the Chinese toward foreigners, all of whom were generally referred to as barbarians. After China's defeat by the British in the Opium Wars of the mid-nineteenth century, some Chinese officials began to recognize the need to study Western military technology, while continuing to assert the superiority of Chinese culture. But, after suffering repeated defeats at the hands of the Western powers, many Chinese began to question the efficacy of their culture or to seek ways to preserve their cultural identity while adopting Western ideas and technology. This issue continued to resurface throughout the nineteenth and twentieth centuries. The abortive "spiritual pollution" campaign of 1983, aimed at eliminating unwanted Western cultural influences, was the most recent manifestation of this dilemma.

Mary Wright, in her essay, shows how the nationalist and anti-foreign sentiments that emerged in the nineteenth century became a potent force in the twentieth century as China faced the prospect of dismemberment at the hands of foreign imperialist powers. Outlining the epochal changes that occurred in China from 1900–50, when political instability, civil war, and foreign invasion racked the country, she notes that China was struck by "equivalents of the Reformation, French Revolution, and Russian Revolution." In the countryside the peasantry suffered from the dual threat of higher taxes and declining income. The success of the Communist Party resulted from the Communists' ability to mobilize the peasantry under the banners of nationalism and social reform. In urban China, Chinese entrepreneurs who had experienced success during World War I, when foreign competition abated, suffered at the hands of a predatory government and foreign competitors who enjoyed special privileges. This period also witnessed the spread of popular education and political awareness. Socialism, liberalism, anarchism, and communism all found adherents in China. Military power became an important component in politics, and ultimately the survival of the major contenders for political power, the Guomindang (Kuomintang) and the Communist Party, was due in part to their command of potent military forces.

The video "Remembering" focuses on the importance of the imperial institution in Chinese history and its role in the continuity of Chinese culture. From 221 B.C., when the emperor Qin Shihuangdi forcibly united the feudal states of ancient China, until the fall of the Qing (Ch'ing) dynasty in 1911, the centralized Chinese state remained consistent in form. Yet despite the fact that China was a centralized bureaucratic state in which the emperor wielded absolute power, there were also de facto limits on imperial power that are not evident in the video. Prior to the Song dynasty the government was staffed by large landholders who traced their orgins to the aristocratic families of feudal China. Political alliances among these families often served to check imperial power. During the Tang dynasty (618–906) the power of local military governors challenged imperial authority. During the Ming dynasty (1368–1644) imperial power was further concentrated in the hands of the emperor, but the burdens of governing led to a reliance on palace eunuchs capable of manipulating the emperor. Similarly, bureaucratic inertia often thwarted imperial initiatives. Still, the underlying trend in Chinese history was toward greater concentration of power in the hands of the emperor.

Much of the video is devoted to assessing the political legacy of Mao Zedong. In showing the devastating effects of the Great Leap Forward, the excesses of the Cultural Revolution, and the near deification of Mao, the video casts Mao as a latter-day emperor whose arbitrary use of power and pursuit of his own failed policies plunged China into chaos. He is compared in particular to Qin Shihuangdi, whose unification of China was achieved at a terrible human cost. Mao's antipathy toward intellectuals is also compared to that of Qin. While it may be possible to compare Mao to a traditional emperor in terms of his use of political power, the student should think carefully about whether the analogy is valid in terms of goals and political rationale. It should be considered—as Murphey points out in his introduction and as will become even more apparent in Part Two of this course—that Mao's own thinking and policies changed over the nearly twenty years he was in power. His political thought was based on Marxist-Leninist doctrines; he saw his task as the transformation of a traditional agrarian society along socialist lines, while resisting both the external threat of

militant imperialists and the internal threat of opponents to revolutionary change. His early success as a revolutionary leader was
based on his ability to adapt Marxist-Leninist doctrines to Chinese
circumstances. He turned on the intellectuals only when he saw
them as an obstacle to achieving his vision of socialism. In the end
he attacked all aspects of traditional culture; Mao sought to reorganize society and remold the national consciousness. No Chinese
emperor ever undertook so daunting a task, and no Chinese
emperor ever sought to attack the very foundations of the society
and the polity. As Murphey concludes, China continues to pay a
price for the failures that began with the Great Leap Forward, but
"much constructive work was done; the revolution was far from
being all bad."

Key Concepts

The "Great Tradition." The Great Tradition generally refers to
China's aristocratic tradition, which was transmitted through Confucianism. It is often contrasted with the "Small Tradition," a combination of Daoism, Buddhism, and popular religious beliefs, as they
were practiced by the common people.

Dynasty. A dynasty took its name from a sequence of rulers from
the same patrilineal family. For over 2,000 years China was ruled
by a series of dynasties. (See Alasdair Clayre, pages xi-xiii, for a
list of the various dynasties.)

Mandate of Heaven. The concept of the mandate of heaven was
originally formulated in the tenth century B.C. by the Confucian
scholar, Mencius. The Chinese believed that the virtue of an
emperor was the ethical sanction for maintaining his rule. Bad conduct on the emperor's part removed the sanction and justified rebel-
lion.

Li. The Confucian concept *li* literally means rites, but it included all
those traditional forms that provided an objective standard of conduct. It has the general meaning of decorum or moral behavior according to status.

Legalism. The doctrine of Legalism, which supplied the political
rationale of the Qin dynasty (221–207 B.C.), stressed the rational

organization of society and resources to strengthen the state. It also held that human nature was evil and that exhaustive laws and severe punishments were necessary to expand state power and to keep people submissive and disciplined.

Scholar-gentry. Many Western sinologists have adopted the term scholar-gentry to describe the elite intelligentsia who were the primary source of government officials in traditional China. This term reflects the fact that the power of this group was based on a combination of their educational attainments and on their economic power as landholders.

Century of Humiliation. The Chinese sometimes refer to the years from 1842 to 1949 as the century of humiliation. Beginning with the Opium War in 1842, foreign imperialist powers used military force, or the threat of force, to expand the areas of China open to foreign trade and missionary work. In the process China was compelled to accept a series of treaties which granted unequal economic and judicial rights to foreigners residing in China.

Republican Revolution of 1911. Prior to 1911 a variety of political factions loosely united under the "Revolutionary Alliance" (Tongmenghui) sought to overthrow the Qing dynasty (1644–1911). In 1911 government troops in Wuhan revolted and seized control of the city. This precipitated the defection of troops in other provinces and eventually led to the abdication of the emperor and the establishment of the republic in 1912.

May Fourth Movement. On 4 May 1919 Chinese students in Beijing held major demonstrations to protest the government's acceptance of provisions in the Versailles Treaty granting Germany's former concessions in Shandong province to Japan. The movement quickly spread throughout China's major cities, involving merchants, workers, and intellectuals. The resulting boycott of foreign goods has been acclaimed as the first nationwide expression of Chinese nationalism.

Guomindang. Following the 1911 Revolution, the "Revolutionary Alliance" (Tongmenghui) was reorganized to form the Guomindang, or Nationalist Party. Originally it was a loosely organized political party representing a variety of viewpoints, though largely following the leadership of Sun Yat-sen. During the early 1920s, when the

Guomindang formed a temporary united front with the Chinese Communists, the party was reorganized under strict Leninist lines. Under Guomindang leadership, China was formally unified in 1927. Also in 1927, the Guomindang and the Communists split and remained open adversaries until 1936, when they formed an uneasy alliance against the Japanese that lasted until the end of World War II. After the war open hostilities broke out; following the Communist victory in 1949, the Guomindang leadership moved to Taiwan, where it still exists today.

Great Leap Forward. Dissatisfied with the lack of progress in the socialist transformation of Chinese society, in 1958 Mao Zedong launched an ambitious campaign known as the Great Leap Forward. The Great Leap Forward stressed mass mobilization, political education, and self-reliance and was designed to increase agricultural and industrial productivity while simultaneously reorganizing society. Poor planning, the withdrawal of economic aid from the Soviet Union, and bad weather doomed the Great Leap Forward to failure and led to severe famine in some regions of China.

Cultural Revolution. The Cultural Revolution was a major sociopolitical upheaval that affected all aspects of life in China for nearly a decade. Mao Zedong launched the Cultural Revolution in 1966 as a means to realize his own vision of socialist modernization. The Cultural Revolution began as a debate in literary circles but it soon spread to a criticism of all remnants of Chinese tradition. It became a mass movement led by Chinese youth who took the writings of Mao as their guide. Individuals, especially intellectuals, were physically attacked and were sent to the countryside to learn from the peasants. Eventually the army had to be called in to restore order. The movement was also a political struggle employed by Mao to eliminate from power many of his political rivals. During the Cultural Revolution party and government administration was reorganized to include more workers and peasants in an effort to blunt the influence of intellectuals and to overturn the staus quo which Mao felt was inhibiting the development of socialism in China. During this period, most major universities and schools were closed and, consequently, an entire generation of Chinese youth never received a proper education. The present leadership, many of whom were victims of the Cultural Revolution, have repudiated the movement and now refer to it as the "ten years of disorder."

Review Questions

1. What was the state of Chinese civilization in 2000 B.C., according to Murphey's introduction to Part One?

2. What is the origin of our word "China," and why is it an appropriate term, according to Murphey?

3. As discussed in the Fairbank article, "The Old Order," what are:

   • the Chinese view of the human relationship to nature?

   • the "Mandate of Heaven" and its political applications?

   • the Confucian understanding of human nature?

   How do these find expression in the Confucian ideal of "good government"?

4. What factors spurred the development of the Chinese bureaucracy, and what were its essential administrative principles, according to Fairbank?

5. According to Kracke, what factors caused the population shift during the Song period, and what were the economic and social consequences?

6. What impact did the expansion of cities have on Chinese culture in the Song period?

7. As reflected in the documents on China's response to the West, what were the changing attitudes of the Chinese toward foreigners in the nineteenth century?

8. What are the roots of Chinese nationalism, as discussed by Wright, and what was the role of nationalism in the eventual victory of the Communist revolution?

9. What are some of the misconceptions about China often held by Westerners, according to Wright?

10. Why have the Great Wall and the Forbidden City been such important symbols in China, according to the video?

11. What have been the traumantic events of Chinese history in the last fifty years, as presented in the video?

12. What was the Cultural Revolution—its aims, methods, and effects?

UNIT TWO: GEOGRAPHIC AND ETHNIC DIVERSITY

Study Components

Video: "Eating"

The Heart of the Dragon, by Alasdair Clayre: Chapter Five, "Eating"

Readings from *The Chinese*: Introduction to Part One and Chapter Two, "Geographic and Ethnic Diversity"

1. "The Chinese Scene," by John K. Fairbank

2. "Man and Nature in China," by Rhoads Murphey

3. "Patterns of Nature and Man," by R. R. C. de Crespigny

4. "Regional Urbanization in Nineteenth-Century China," by G. William Skinner

5. "City as a Mirror of Society," by Rhoads Murphey

Learning Objectives

To become acquainted with:

— the major physiographic regions of China

— the geographic and ethnic diversity of China

— Chinese attitudes toward nature and the individual

— patterns of urbanization and regional development

— the variety and abundance of Chinese cuisine

— the insecurity of the food supply, the preoccupation with food, and the ritual quality of eating

Overview

Despite enormous geographic and ethnic diversity, the Chinese have maintained a remarkable degree of political and cultural unity in historical and contemporary times. The articles by Fairbank and de Crespigny provide a neat summary of these variations, particularly the contrast between north and south. The Yangzi river serves as a dividing line between the arid plains of northern China and the lush river valleys of the south. As we see in the video "Eating," environmental factors have shaped the life-styles of the Chinese people. The need to feed a large population has conditioned the form and intensity of Chinese agriculture. There is roughly less than one-half acre of food-producing soil per person and little room for expansion. Thus, the emphasis is on grain production, with only a minimal amount of land given over to animal husbandry. Chinese agriculture is very labor intensive. The high yields of the rice-producing regions of southern China require huge inputs of human labor. Because the task of transplanting rice seedlings is so delicate, suitable mechanization has not yet been developed. The social costs of mechanization would also be great, since there would be few outlets for the surplus labor that mechanization would create. De Crespigny echoes many of Fairbank's points while providing a more technical description of the mountain ranges and rivers of China.

Centuries of intensive agriculture have altered the physiographic features of China but, as Rhoads Murphey notes in "Man and Nature in China," the Chinese approach to nature differs markedly from that of Western nations. The Chinese conceive of human beings as part of a grander natural order, and agricultural practices are designed to maximize the use of natural processes. The natural environment has been altered to supply humans with sustenance, but this has been done in cooperation with nature. This respect for nature is evident in Chinese art and literature, which portray nature in a reverent context. The rewards in high yields and bountiful harvests accruing to the traditional Chinese agriculturalists' harmonious utilization of natural resources no doubt reinforced this cooperative approach to nature. Murphey goes on to note that in modern China nature has been "dethroned" and a confident, pioneering, creative communist individual put in its place. The mobilization of labor has had both economic and political objectives. Economically, the Chinese continue to achieve greater yields from existing resources. Politically, the Communist Party uses mass mobilization to instill political values.

G. William Skinner is an anthropologist whose regional analysis of Chinese urbanization has had a great influence on Western studies of Chinese society, polity, and economy. Relating historical development to geography, Skinner defines nine physiographic regions in China within which discrete urban networks were formed. Within these regions resources of all kinds—social, cultural, economic, and political—were utilized and exploited. By dividing China into these nine macroregions, Skinner supplies a useful tool of analysis which helps explain the variation in historical cycles of regional development.

While Skinner's article explains the urbanization process in nineteenth-century China, Rhoads Murphey's second article discusses urbanization as a reflection of Chinese cultural values in both imperial and contemporary times. Cities were primarily centers of imperial authority, and as such were symbols of Confucian virtues of order designed to project imperial power into the countryside. The county (xian) level capitals were carefully laid out in a precise geometric fashion. Imposed on a varied landscape, county capitals were designed to control and tax the countryside, the source of wealth in an agrarian society. Unlike Western cities, they did not serve as political centers which could potentially challenge imperial authority. Similarly, there was no contempt on the part of city dwellers for rural people, and rural people were held in high esteem.

Many Chinese elites were themselves natives of the countryside and kept close ties with their native villages.

The video "Eating" and Clayre's chapter "Eating" offer close-ups of Chinese cuisine that further illustrate the geographic diversity, regional contrasts, and the ongoing struggle to feed an ever-growing population. Beginning in southern China, where culinary arts are most highly developed, we see the art of Chinese cooking at its best. Many foreigners find Chinese food exotic, but even the Chinese themselves are awed by the strangeness of some Cantonese dishes. Recent economic reforms in China have allowed for the establishment of small-scale private enterprises, and some of the most successful have been the family-run restaurants, such as that of the chicken seller shown in the video. Still, as the narrator remarks, the elaborate feasting pictured in the video is not the norm. Banquets are special occasions, and the typical Chinese family continues to subsist on more simple fare like the meal of the Muslim family of north China. Despite the penchant for elaborate feasting, the burdens of a vast population and the intensity of Chinese agriculture limit the degree to which the Chinese can indulge themselves.

Chinese civilization has survived in part because of the enormous resourcefulness and hard work of Chinese farmers. This theme is reiterated in the video and readings. The monumental irrigation works and the terracing of mountainsides are striking examples of how the Chinese have altered their environment. When nature cannot be harnessed to serve man, technology must be developed to make the best of limited resources. The Chinese cooking pan, the wok, and the practice of carefully slicing ingredients before cooking are designed to minimize the amount of fuel used to prepare food. Also significant is the Chinese attitude toward food, which, as Clayre and the video clearly illustrate, has a ritualized quality that stems from a memory of past periods of scarcity and famine.

Key Concepts

China Proper. The term China Proper generally refers to those provinces of China which historically formed the core of the Chinese empire. They include the present day provinces of Hebei, Henan, Shaanxi, Shanxi, Gansu, Shandong, Hubei, Hunan, Jiangsu, Zhejiang, Fujian, Taiwan, Guangdong, Guangxi, Yunnan, Guizhou,

Sichuan, Anhui, and Jiangxi. (See the map in *The Heart of the Dragon.*)

Outer Areas. Tibet, Xinjiang, Mongolia, and Manchuria are sometimes referred to as outer areas. Each of these regions contains large populations of ethnic minorities. Historically they were not always incorporated into the Chinese empire.

Autonomous Regions. Very soon after the establishment of the People's Republic of China, autonomous administrative units were organized at all levels of administration in areas inhabited by minority nationalities. National autonomous areas include autonomous regions, autonomous prefectures, autonomous *xian* (counties), and autonomous banners. First-order autonomous regions are the largest and include the Inner Mongolian Autonomous Region, the Xinjiang Uighur Autonomous Region, the Guangxi Zhuang Autonomous Region, the Ningxia Hui Autonomous Region, and the Tibetian Autonomous Region. All autonomous regions, regardless of size, are completely integrated into the regular centralized administrative hierarchy. They have neither more nor less authority than regular administrative units and differ only in that concessions are made to local minority customs and language and that a special effort is made to integrate minority cadres into the administrative structure.

Review Questions

1. According to Murphey's introduction to Part One, what is the distinction between "China Proper" and the outer areas, and what have been the relations between them?

2. What are the major regional contrasts in China, as discussed by Murphey in the introduction and by Fairbank in Chapter Two? What are the basic geographic and climatic effects?

3. According to Fairbank, how has the physical environment of China shaped the "distinctly Chinese way of life"?

4. What is the difference between the traditional Chinese attitude toward nature and the attitude since the revolution of 1949, as discussed by Murphey in "Man and Nature in China"? How do these attitudes compare with those in the West?

5. What are the reasons for the revolutionary change in attitude toward the natural world in the People's Republic? What are some of the benefits and risks of the new attitude, as described by Murphey?

6. As presented by de Crespigny, what are the major topographical features of China? What are China's major crops and industrial resources?

7. Why does Skinner use a regional approach to understanding urbanization in nineteenth-century China?

8. What does Skinner define as the determining factors for the location of regional "cores"?

9. What were the actual and symbolic roles of China's cities in imperial times, as discussed by Murphey in "City as a Mirror of Society"? How did they mirror the values of imperial China? How do China's modern cities reflect contemporary goals and values?

10. According to Murphey, what was the traditionally perceived relationship between city and countryside in China? What have been the attitudes toward cities under different Communist leaders?

11. What is revealed in the video "Eating" about how China's geographical and climatic diversity affects the life-styles of different regions?

12. From the evidence in the video, what is the Chinese attitude toward food? Why has food always been such a preoccupation? What have been the major problems of food production, and how have the Chinese dealt with them?

PART ONE:
ESSAY/DISCUSSION QUESTIONS

1. What factors have contributed to China's political and cultural unity?

Suggested Guidelines:

a. Consider the Confucian tradition, referring especially to:

   ● Murphey's introductory essay in the Reader

   ● "The Old Order" and "The Chinese Scene" by Fairbank in the Reader and the role of Confucian ideology and Chinese attitudes toward nature and the individual

b. Examine the imperial tradition, with reference to:

   ● the video "Remembering" and Clayre's chapter "Remembering" in *The Heart of the Dragon*, examining the historical background and evaluating the strengths of the imperial tradition

   ● the video "Remembering" and Fairbank's treatment in the Reader of the concept "Mandate of Heaven," the role of the emperor, and the nature of the bureaucratic order that stemmed from "imperial Confucianism"

   ● the introduction to Part One in the Reader, the video "Remembering," and Clayre's first chapter on the achievements of the Qin (Ch'in) and Han dynasties, and the historical and continuing role of a strong, centralized government

   ● the Kracke selection in the Reader on the precedent for "change within tradition"

c. Consider historical consciousness in China, referring to:

- the introduction to Part One and the documents about China's response to the West in the Reader, and the video "Remembering," concerning Chinese pride in the imperial idea and Chinese civilization

- the Wright article in the Reader and the video "Remembering," concerning the significance of nationalism

d. Consider the importance of language, as discussed in Murphey's introductory essay to Part One in the Reader.

2. What geographic and political factors have exerted pressures against the maintenance of a unitary Chinese state?

Suggested Guidelines:

a. Review China's geography, referring to:

- Murphey's introduction to Part One and the selections by Fairbank and de Crespigny in Chapter Two of the Reader, concerning major regional contrasts and physical barriers between some regions

- Clayre's discussion in "Living" (pages 129–40) in *The Heart of the Dragon*

- the video "Eating" and Clayre's chapter "Eating," on how regional differences have affected life-styles and cultures

- Murphey's discussion in his introduction to Part One of the Reader on the ethnic and cultural variations in China and the distinction between China Proper and the Outer Areas

- Skinner's discussion of regionalism and de Crespigny's account of the geographic factors affecting changes in political power bases, both in the Reader

b. Consider the political factors that have encouraged disunity, referring to:

- Murphey's introduction to Part One in the Reader, and Clayre's chapter and the video, both entitled "Remembering," concerning the history and political styles of different dynasties; rebellions; foreign pressure, invasion, rule, and "spheres of influence"; and differing attitudes toward reform held by the Nationalists and the Communists

- de Crespigny's view of the constraints on modernization, in the Reader

- the divisions caused among the people by changing attitudes toward nature and modernization, as outlined by Murphey in "Man and Nature" in the Reader

- Murphey's discussion in "Cities as a Mirror of Society" in the Reader of the traditional relationship between urban and rural areas, and the changes since 1949

Part Two
Politics

Part Two introduces a political tradition that is more than 2,000 years old. This section of the course discusses the political systems of both traditional and contemporary China, examining political thought, national political institutions, and the interaction between the political system and the individual.

UNIT THREE: IDEOLOGY AND ORGANIZATION

Study Components

Video: "Believing"

The Heart of the Dragon, by Alasdair Clayre: Chapter Two, "Believing"

Readings from *The Chinese*: Introduction to Part Two and Chapter Three, "Ideology and Organization"

1. "Sources of Chinese Tradition," by Confucius, Mencius, and Han Fei

2. "The Political Tradition," by John K. Fairbank

3. "The Chinese Revolution," by Mao Zedong

4. "The Constitution of the Communist Party of China, 1982"

5. "China After Mao," by Steven M. Goldstein, Kathrin Sears, and Richard C. Bush

6. "China's Political Evolution: 1972–82," by Michel Oksenberg and Richard Bush

Learning Objectives

To become acquainted with:

— the principal tenets of traditional Chinese religious and ethical beliefs

— the Confucian and Legalist political tradition

— the structure of political organization in modern China and its historical antecedents

— some basic principles of Mao Zedong Thought

— political developments in China since the death of Mao Zedong

— the challenges posed to Communist ideology by new efforts to improve material well-being

Overview

Some aspects of the Chinese political system have already been touched on in the video "Remembering" and in Part One of *The Chinese*, but this unit of the course examines more systematically the political thought and organization of China. Since the establishment of the People's Republic of China in 1949, Marxism-Leninism and Mao Zedong Thought together have been the official ideology of China. Chapter Three of *The Chinese* investigates both the recent challenges to the current political orthodoxy and the political and religious beliefs of the past, which continue to influence political thought in China. Chapter Two of *The Heart of the Dragon* by Alasdair Clayre and the video "Believing" provide a general survey of the basic tenets of traditional ethical and religious beliefs.

Three major branches of thought—Confucianism, which expounded a code of moral conduct; Daoism, a uniquely Chinese
religion emphasizing harmony with nature; and Buddhism, which
offers a path to salvation and the promise of an afterlife—have all
coexisted for centuries and continue to influence Chinese culture.
The durability of these three diverse belief systems and their continued influence on Chinese thought are testimony to the practical
and eclectic approach to religion that the Chinese have evinced
throughout their history. Also important are the numerous popular
religious beliefs, frequently based on local superstitions or legends.
These popular beliefs provided solace to the masses and in times of
political turmoil served to unify peasant rebellions.

Confucianism was the official political ideology of China from
the Han dynasty (206 B.C.–220 A.D.) until the Revolution of 1911.
Prior to the Han dynasty the doctrine of Legalism, which was
favored by Qin Shihuangdi, the first unifier of China, was a potent
competitor to Confucianism. The excerpts in "Sources of Chinese
Tradition" highlight the major differences between these two schools
of thought. Although Confucianism eventually triumphed, elements
of Legalism were incorporated into it to strengthen the structure of
bureaucratic rule.

The political organization of traditional China is outlined in John
Fairbank's article. As he notes, although the emperor retained absolute power, the government was administered by a centralized
bureaucracy. At the national level, government administration was
in the hands of the Six Boards and, in descending order, provincial
governors and county magistrates. Beneath the county level, formal administration was virtually nonexistent and local problems
were often handled by resident members of the scholar gentry,
whose prestige was based on a combination of economic power and
educational attainment. The formal governmental structure was
carefully delineated, with forms of communication, terms of office,
and administrative rankings all rigidly defined.

Mao Zedong assumed the leadership of the Chinese Communist
Party during the 1930s, and his political thought remains an integral component of official Chinese ideology. The Reader contains
some excerpts from Mao's writings which illustrate both the consis-
tency and flexibility of Mao's thought. In the first excerpt Mao explains the policy of New Democracy, which was intended to be a
prefatory stage for the development of socialism. It is very important to consider New Democracy in its historical context. In 1947
the Communist Party was still engaged in a civil war with the

Guomindang government, and support from non-Communist elements was considered essential to the success of the revolution. Thus, Mao defined the enemies of the revolution in very narrow terms: the feudal landlord class and monopoly capitalists. Middle peasants and the national bourgeoisie were assured of a place in the political order, but the supremacy of the Communist Party, the leadership of the proletariat and the peasants, and the eventual goal of socialism were also clearly stated. The second and third excerpts were written during the late 1950s, after the Communist Party had consolidated its power. These writings reflect Mao's dissatisfaction with the pace of the socialist transformation of Chinese society and his disenchantment with the Soviet model of development. Thus, Mao espoused a theory of "permanent revolution," criticizing the blind copying of the Soviet Union and urging a rapid and continual advance toward socialism. Mao's goal, a socialist society, remained consistent but his strategy for achieving this goal had changed. Similarly, the present regime has rejected many of Mao's strategies, but, as stated in the Constitution of 1982 in Chapter Three of the Reader, Mao's thought remains a key component of Chinese ideology.

Goldstein, Sears, and Bush describe the current political organization of the People's Republic of China. This structure follows the Soviet model, with the Communist Party hierarchy mirroring governmental organization. Most major decisions are made in executive committees according to Marxist-Leninist principles of democratic centralism. Representative bodies exist, but their function is to ratify decisions of the executive committees. Policy is implemented through the bureaucracy, which at times has proved unresponsive or obstructionist. The age-old problems of the bureaucratic state—nepotism, corruption, and bureaucratic foot-dragging—persist and, some say, have been exacerbated by the sudden policy shifts that characterized the Cultural Revolution.

In the post-Mao era, China's leadership has adopted a new strategy designed to achieve modernization by the year 2000. Oksenberg and Bush provide some excellent insights into the elite political struggles from 1972–82 that produced these policy changes. These shifts are apparent in the new Constitution of the Communist Party of 1982, which marks an official retreat from the ideological fervor of the Maoist era and places a renewed emphasis on improving material well-being. Despite the apparent victory of Deng Xiaoping and the "authoritarian reformers" who support him, the legacy of Mao's rule survives and continues to pose an obstacle to reform. The emphasis on improving the living standards of the people also poses the additional problem of tailoring ideology to achieve new goals. In the video, the brigade leader from Shandong, Zhao Kuisheng, expresses the concern of many Communist leaders when he laments the apparent materialism which seems to have taken hold of China's younger generation.

The problem of maintaining ideological awareness while pursuing a modernization program designed to raise living standards may pose the greatest challenge to China's Communist leadership. The theory of "permanent revolution" and the distrust of expertise put forth by Mao in the 1950s has been discredited, but not entirely repudiated. New policies encourage people to get rich, but they also recognize that some will prosper more than others. The spirit of self-sacrifice developed during the era of revolutionary struggle, which sustained earlier generations, is alien to today's youth. In opposition, we see in the video the survival of such old beliefs as offerings to the fertility goddess of Taishan. Also, the opening to the outside world, which is part of the policy of modernization, may mean the introduction of new, and perhaps more disruptive, ideologies. It is unclear how the present leadership will deal with these ideological challenges or with the potential conflict that widening gaps in living standards will pose.

Key Concepts

Li. See Unit One.

Legalism. See Unit One.

The Five Relationships. The five relationships and their appropriate forms are affection between parent and child; righteousness between ruler and subject; distinction between husband and wife; order between old and young; and sincerity between friends. The five relationships comprise the central values of Confucian society.

Daoism. In its original form Daoism was a philosophical system deriving chiefly from the *Daodejing*, a book traditionally ascribed to Laozi. It describes the individual's ideal state as freedom from desire and a life of effortless simplicity, achieved by following the Dao (the Way), the spontaneous creative functioning of the universe. Quietistic in nature, Daoists condemned the social virtues expounded by Confucius. Later Daoism stressed the search for immortality, supposed to flow from the Dao, and also encouraged the practice of alchemy. By the fifth century A.D., Daoism had incorporated many elements of Mahayana Buddhism and offered a more developed religious system.

The New Democratic Revolution. Mao devised the theory of the New Democratic Revolution during the Sino-Japanese War. According to this theory, the Communist Party would assume the leadership of a broad united front of all revolutionary elements: workers, peasants, and segments of the middle class. The purpose of the New Democratic Revolution was the defeat of foreign aggressors and the overthrow of reactionary elements at home. The New Democratic Revolution emphasized anti-imperialism, honest government, and socioeconomic reform while downplaying class struggle. This policy was designed to garner broad support during the later stages of the revolution and the early years of the People's Republic of China, but Mao always maintained that the New Democratic Revolution was merely a preparatory stage that would eventually give way to a socialist revolution, which could only be accomplished under the leadership of the Communist Party.

Permanent Revolution. In the late 1950s Mao became increasingly concerned that the emphasis on economic growth was leading to a degeneration of revolutionary values, complacency among Chinese bureaucrats, and the reemergence of class enemies in society. Thus, despite the establishment of a socialist society, nonantagonistic contradictions continued to exist. Mao's response was the theory of "permanent revolution," which emphasized the mobilization and politicization of the masses, struggle against intellectuals and technical specialists, and a general emphasis on revolutionary egalitarianism. These policies were hallmarks of the Great Leap Forward and the Cultural Revolution.

Constitution of 1982. The Constitution of 1982, written under the guidance of Deng Xiaoping and his reformist supporters, represents a rejection of the more radical policies of the Maoist era. It criticizes the emphasis on class struggle and distrust of intellectuals and stresses economic growth and improved standards of living. Excerpts from the preamble of the Constitution of 1982 are reprinted in Chapter Three.

Dual System of Party and State. In China, as in other Communist countries, the Communist Party organization parallels the formal government apparatus. Most major political descisions are made within Party organs, but these decisions are implemented through the state apparatus under the supervision of the Party.

Cadre. In every major political, economic, and cultural unit in China there are cadres, Communist Party members responsible for organizing the unit and implementing party policies.

The Four Modernizations. The Four Modernizations is the policy to modernize agriculture, industry, science and technology, and national defense by the year 2000. It was originally proposed by Hua Guofeng, Mao's successor. Hua has since been eased from power, but the policy of the Four Modernizations has been retained.

Review Questions

1. What were the factors involved in the decay of China's traditional system of government, according to Goldstein's introduction to Part Two in the Reader?

2. What adaptations did Mao make in Marxist-Leninist theory, according to Goldstein?

3. What are the different points of view about human nature expressed in the selections from "Sources of Chinese Tradition"?

4. What are the main differences in political philosophy between the Confucians and the Legalists?

5. According to Fairbank, what was the basic organization of the imperial bureaucracy, and how was centralized control maintained?

6. As described by Fairbank, who were the Chinese gentry, why were they important to the imperial government, and what were their functions?

7. What is the difference in emphasis between Mao's 1947 speech and his later speeches, as included in the Reader?

8. What is Mao's theory of permanent revolution or continuous struggle?

9. What is the principal contradiction in Chinese society, according to the Preamble of the 1982 Constitution of the Communist Party?

10. As outlined by Goldstein, Sears, and Bush, what are the two parts of the Chinese political structure, and what are the organizational levels of administration?

11. What problems in the bureaucracy is the Deng government trying to correct, as discussed by Goldstein et al?

12. In addition to "spectacular events," Oksenberg and Bush name seven significant "quiet developments" that are especially important in China's political evolution. What are they?

13. According to Oksenberg and Bush, what are the stages of evolution in the Chinese system in the years 1972–82?

14. On what grounds do Oksenberg and Bush determine that a political equilibrium has not yet been reached?

15. As presented in the video "Believing" and in Clayre's chapter of the same title, what are the major tenets of Buddhism, Daoism, Confucianism, and popular Chinese religions?

16. As illustrated in the video, how did Mr. Zhao's attitudes toward traditional religion change, and for what reasons?

17. What values do traditional Chinese beliefs and Communism seem to have in common, according to the video presentation?

18. What problems have been generated by the Cultural Revolution and by the new prosperity?

UNIT FOUR: THE INDIVIDUAL AND THE STATE

Study Components

Video: "Correcting"

The Heart of the Dragon, by Alasdair Clayre: Chapter Eight, "Correcting"

Readings from *The Chinese*: Introduction to Part Two and Chapter Four, "The Individual and the State"

1. "Two Models of Law," by Victor H. Li

2. "Law in Imperial China: Cases from the *Hsing-an Hui-lan*," with commentary by Derk Bodde and Clarence Morris

3. "Mr. Wang vs. Mr Chen: A High Ch'ing Parable," by Frederic Wakeman, Jr.

4. "The One Who Loved Dog Meat," by B. Michael Frolic

5. "Prisoners of Conscience and the Death Penalty," by Amnesty International

6. "Political Participation in Communist China," by James R. Townsend

7. "A Cadre's Land Reform Diary," by Chang Su

Learning Objectives

To become acquainted with:

— aspects of the traditional Chinese legal system

— the evolution and development of the Chinese legal system since 1949

— the present procedures of criminal prosecution and the goals and methods of the penal system

— the fate of Chinese political and religious dissidents

— the nature and meaning of political participation in China

Overview

In exploring the interaction between the individual and the state in China, this unit focuses on the legal system, which even in its contemporary form retains influences from past ideologies, and on the nature and extent of political participation.

Historically, the Chinese have had an ambivalent attitude toward law. As seen in the previous chapter, Confucianism, as developed by Mencius, stressed the innate goodness and perfectibility of the individual. Proper education would ensure that people would accept and act according to their respective roles and responsibilities in the social hierarchy, thereby making codified law unnecessary. Thus, although courts of law existed, numerous proverbs can be cited to illustrate the popular fear of litigation and to show that private mediation was the preferred method of conflict resolution. Not all disputes could be handled in this fashion, however, and, by the Tang dynasty (618–908), the Chinese had established a detailed law code, which became a model for many other Asian countries.

The hypothetical case of Mr. Wang versus Mr. Chen, discussed by Frederic Wakeman, illustrates one reason why the average citizen of imperial China was reluctant to resort to litigation. An individual's standing in society was often more important than the merits of the suit he or she might bring before the magistrate.

Nevertheless, the administration of justice in imperial China was not entirely arbitrary. The examples presented in the reading by Bodde and Morris were precedent-setting cases taken from a Qing dynasty (1644–1911) handbook for magistrates. Once a case made its way into the official legal system, investigations were painstakingly thorough. Criminal cases were regarded as disruptions of the natural social harmony, and precise punishments were required to restore that harmony. Since cases involving homicide were automatically reviewed by higher authorities, local magistrates were very careful in their deliberations and verdicts.

Since 1949 the Chinese legal system has undergone several reforms. According to Victor Li, the Chinese legal system has alternated between an "external" and "internal" model. This dichotomy is indicative of the changing political currents and also reflects the historical Chinese ambivalence toward the use of formal law. An example of the internal model, which relies on social pressure for enforcement, is the land reform program discussed in Chapter Eight of *The Heart of the Dragon* and described in "A Cadre's Land Reform Diary" by Chang Su, a cadre who participated in land reform in Sichuan province. The external model, which more closely resembles a Western-style legal system, has recently been reinstated in reaction to the abuses of the politicized people's courts of the Cultural Revolution era.

The video "Correcting" examines the workings of China's reformed legal system. Elements of Western-style judicature are apparent, but the emphasis on the social context of the crime, the need to reeducate the criminal, and the effects of the crime on the accused's family reflect traditional Chinese concerns. Defense attorneys do not assume the adversarial role of their Western counterparts, as is evident by the judge's impatience with the arguments of the defense attorney. By the time the case reaches trial, the only outstanding issue seems to be sentencing. Contrite offenders are more likely to receive lenient sentences, and it seems that there is little to be gained from resisting authority. As we learn from B. Michael Frolic's reading, this is true of the penal system as well. Evidence of rehabilitation is very important, and prison authorities can extend the sentences of recalcitrant offenders.

Whatever its faults, the present legal system represents some improvement over the recent past. Still, as the Amnesty International Report indicates, political cases continue to be handled differently from ordinary criminal cases. Control of the judicial system remains in the hands of the Communist Party, and political dissidents are frequently detained without trial. The extensive use of the death penalty during a recent "law and order" campaign also serves as a reminder that the administration of justice is not immune from politics.

The Amnesty International Report also raises questions about political participation in China. Townsend's essay addresses this issue and points out how it differs from the Western democratic model of political participation. Since 1949 political participation has increased significantly compared to that of imperial times. Nevertheless, political participation remains limited to officially sanctioned activities. Political campaigns are orchestrated from above and are designed to carry out party policy. When party policy coincides with popular interests, as in the case of the land reform program described by Chang Su, popular response has been enthusiastic. Unpopular campaigns, however, are sometimes met with resistance, as with the party's birth control campaign, described by Mosher in Chapter Seven.

Key Concepts

"Internal" and "External" Models of Law. Victor Li's article in Chapter Four describes the development of the post-1949 system in terms of the competion between two models of law. The internal model, which resembles the Confucian concept of law, relies on moral suasion and education. The external model, resembling the Legalist approach to law, is based on formal, written legal codes.

Political Participation. The nature of political participation in China, the involvement of the ordinary citizen in the political process, is very different from our Western notion. In China participation consists of taking part in the implementation of predetermined policies. The process of political participation is meant to educate citizens in the goals and aspirations of the regime and to create a motivated citizenry which accepts the basic policies of the regime through their involvement in their implementation.

Review Questions

1. What did the saying "heaven is high and the emperor is far away" imply about the relationship of most Chinese to politics?

2. Give some examples of the successes and failures of the Chinese Communists' attempts to encourage political participation.

3. What does Victor Li mean when he refers to the "internal" and the "external" models of law? What are the basic rationales and objectives of each model?

4. How do these models of law co-exist, and even complement each other?

5. In the two cases illustrated in "Law in Imperial China," what evidence is there of the application of Confucian principles?

6. What options were open to Mr. Wang and Mr. Ch'en, respectively, in their legal dispute, as told in the parable by Wakeman? How does the outcome reflect the workings of the legal and political system of Qing society?

7. What was the aim of the state's imprisonment of "the one who loved dog meat" and how did this prisoner deal with the system?

8. What contrasts does Townsend make between the Communist Chinese and Western styles of popular political participation?

9. What does Townsend mean by "latent" functions of some social behavior in relation to political participation?

10. How do legal policy and practice sometimes contradict each other, as cited in the Amnesty International

reports of the death penalty and human rights in China?

11. What was the "free speech" or "democracy" movement, and how was it handled by the government, as described in the Amnesty International report?

12. What were the basic stages of the land reform efforts, as related in "The Diary of a Land Reform Cadre"?

13. What were the activities of land reform cadres?

14. In the video "Correcting," what traditional Chinese social values are revealed as still affecting the goals and methods of the legal system? What changes in legal measures have occurred since the Cultural Revolution?

15. What basic differences do you see between our legal system and the Chinese legal system, as shown in the video "Correcting"?

16. As presented in the video, what factors in China's recent political and social history have contributed to the recent increase in crime?

PART TWO: ESSAY/DISCUSSION QUESTIONS

1. In what ways are the traditional political philosophies and structure of China evident in Chinese Communist ideology and government?

Suggested Guidelines:

a. Consider the nature of traditional Chinese society, referring to:

   • the "Sources of Chinese Tradition" selections in the Reader, especially Confucian ideas of self-cultivation, social organization, and the role of government; and Legalist attitudes toward government control and law

- Fairbank's discussion in the Reader of the imperial bureaucracy and its hierarchical structure, and local government, with attention to the balance between centralization and local autonomy

- the articles "Sources of Chinese Tradition" and "Law in Imperial China" in the Reader, particularly as they describe the balance between rule by law and rule by men

- Clayre's chapter "Believing" in *The Heart of the Dragon* on the interplay between religious/philosophical ideas and government

- the video "Believing" and the reasons for Mr. Zhao's transfer of his religious faith to the Communist Party

b. Review the organization of the state since 1949, with reference to:

- Clayre's discussion of Chinese Communism and the tradition of the "great leader," in the chapter "Believing" in *The Heart of the Dragon*

- the introduction to Part Two in the Reader, on political ideology in China since 1949

- Mao's speech in the Reader stating his view of the power of the state in restructuring society; and the Chinese Constitution, also in the Reader, regarding the aim of a "socialist spiritual civilization"

- the video "Believing" on the attitude toward Mao during the Cultural Revolution

- Goldstein et al in the Reader on the hierarchical structure of the dual Party/state system

- Oksenberg and Bush in the Reader regarding Mao's attitude toward bureaucracies, and the Deng-Chen reforms in collective leadership and the rebuilding of political institutions

2. How has the relationship of Chinese citizens to the state continued in traditional ways, and how has it changed since 1949?

Suggested Guidelines:

a. Consider the traditional and modern legal systems, with reference to:

- the introduction to Part Two in the Reader on Confucian and Legalist attitudes toward law, and their past and continuing influence on Chinese law

- Clayre's discussion in the chapter "Correcting" in *The Heart of the Dragon* on the aims, history, and changes in China's legal system

- Victor Li's article in the Reader examining two legal models

- the two imperial law cases included in the Reader and the extent to which they embody Li's models

- "Mr. Wang vs. Mr. Ch'en" in the Reader and the attitudes of the two men toward the workings of the law

- the video "Correcting" and the persistence of traditional values

- the articles "The One Who Loved Dog Meat" and "The Death Penalty," both in the Reader, and the video "Correcting" concerning the aims and methods of the penal system

- the introduction to Part Two and the Amnesty International report in the Reader, the Clayre chapter

"Correcting" in *The Heart of the Dragon*, and the video concerning reforms of the legal system and human rights

b. Examine the state's attitude toward popular political participation, with reference to:

- the introduction to Part Two in the Reader discussing traditional and modern attitudes

- Townsend's article in the Reader analyzing the characteristics of China's current style of political participation

- "A Cadre's Land Reform Diary" in the Reader regarding the Communists' aims in rural areas, with attention to the cadre's response to his activities and to the state's aim in sending urban professionals into the countryside

Part Three
Society

Part Three introduces the basic social organization of both imperial and contemporary China. This section of the course focuses on the family as the basic unit of social life, on broader forms of community that link individuals and families, and on cleavages among different elements in the complex society of China.

UNIT FIVE: THE CHINESE FAMILY

Study Components

Video: "Marrying"

The Heart of the Dragon, by Alasdair Clayre: Chapter Three, "Marrying"

Readings from *The Chinese*: Introduction to Part Two and Chapter Five, "The Chinese Family"

1. "Family Instructions," edited by Patricia B. Ebrey

2. "The Family," by Ba Jin

3. "Urban Workers' Housework," by Wang Yalin and Li Jinrong

4. "Zhao Xiuyin: Lady of the Sties," by Mary Sheridan

5. "Courtship, Love, and Marriage: The Life and Times of Yu Luojin," by Emily Honig

Learning Objectives

To become acquainted with:

— the importance of the family as a social and economic unit

— traditional rules of conduct governing Chinese families

— the strength of traditional moral values and their continuing influence on Chinese families

— Chinese marriage customs and rituals

— the status of women in traditional Chinese society and changes in their status since 1949

— contemporary Chinese attitudes toward the family, marriage, and divorce

— the quality of life in contemporary urban China

Overview

Throughout Chinese history the family has been the most important social and economic unit. Unlike Western societies, where individualism is prized, Chinese society has emphasized the primacy of the family and the obligation of the individual to submerge personal ambition and goals for the sake of the harmony and prosperity of the family. Patricia Ebrey's article on family instructions shows that the rules governing families were extensive. These rules were taken from the preface of a late Ming dynasty (1368–1644) genealogy, but similar rules existed in earlier times and the values expressed in these rules still influence Chinese society. These rules expressed an idealized view of how the family should function, but the prohibitions contained in the rules also indicate the areas of potential conflict within the family.

The excerpt from Ba Jin's (Pa Chin's) novel, *The Family*, which is set in the early twentieth century, illustrates how the needs of the family determined the fate of Kao Chueh-hsin. In keeping with the hierarchical organization of the traditional Chinese family, Chueh-hsin's father and grandfather chose his education, wife, and occupation. Although Chueh-hsin did not welcome these decisions, he submitted to them, sadly, but without objection. Despite Chueh-hsin's lack of freedom, the story seems to indicate that, at least in his marriage, Chueh-hsin was not entirely unhappy.

Wang Yalin and Li Jinrong's report on urban worker's housework details the problems of contemporary life in urban China. Domestic chores continue to consume an incredible amount of time, burdening the personal lives of urban Chinese families, especially the women, and affecting the economy as well. Although the study does not address the issue directly, it would seem to indicate that the family will continue to be an important economic as well as social unit in contemporary China. Aside from the interesting finding contained in this study, it is also significant because it was one of the first empirical sociological studies in China.

Turning to family life, Mary Sheridan provides a poignant portrayal of Zhao Xiuyin, an industrious and intelligent peasant woman. Although Xiuyin was married in 1950 when equality for women had been established by law, pressure from her husband, which Xiuyin attributed to his "feudal attitudes," and the burdens of child rearing prevented her from pursuing a career. Thus, despite official efforts to guarantee equality, traditional attitudes toward women still prevail in rural China, and women, such as Xiuyin, often fail to realize their ambitions. Alasdair Clayre makes the point that equality under the law could be a mixed blessing. Quite often women were expected to undertake the same duties as men in addition to their traditional household work rather than instead of it.

Emily Honig tells the story of Yu Luojin, which depicts not only the persistence of traditional values, but also the changes that have occurred in contemporary Chinese society. Concern for the welfare of her family was an important consideration in Yu Luojin's decisions, though she ultimately did not lose sight of her own goals. Her experiences contrast sharply with those of the traditional Chinese woman Alasdair Clayre describes in *The Heart of Dragon* but they also fall well short of the idyllic picture of marriage in contemporary China portrayed in the video "Marrying." The tyranny of tradition may have been overcome, but Yu Luojin's case shows that in contemporary China politics can, as tradition once did, impinge harshly on the personal choices of Chinese men and women.

The Marriage Law of 1950 ostensibly eliminated many of the traditional marriage customs that discriminated against women. (Alasdair Clayre describes these practices in Chapter Three of *The Heart of the Dragon*.) Most notably it provided for freedom of choice

in marriage and gave women the right to divorce. In the video
"Marrying" we see the effects of these reforms juxtaposed with the
strength of traditional customs. The marriage is one of free choice
but in deference to the bride's mother an intermediary is employed
to obtain her permission. This intermediary also handles the complex negotiations for the gift giving and arrangements for the
elaborate feasting which accompany the wedding ceremony. Also in
accordance with tradition, the bride marries into her husband's
household. Although the relative advances for women have been
among the most revolutionary changes since 1949, the tenacity of
traditional attitudes toward women and the limits of the reform are
evident, to varying degrees, in the video as well as in the lives of
both Zhao Xiuyin and Yu Luojin.

Key Concepts

Filial Piety. Filial piety refers to the first and most important of the
five relationships of Confucianism, which is respect for one's
parents. See "the Five Relationships" in Unit Three.

Lineage. A lineage is a corporate group which celebrates ritual
unity and is based on demonstrated descent from a common ances-
tor. When the line of descent is traced through male members of
the lineage, it is called a patrilineage.

Communes. The commune is the highest administrative unit in
rural China. There were over 50,000 communes in China in 1980.
The average size was 15,000 people or 3,000 families. The commune is responsible for registry of births and marriages, postal services, and police. Most communes also have a clinic and middle
school. The commune also supervises procurement of grain to meet
the state's agricultural delivery obligations and is the locus of political leadership in the countryside.

Production Brigade. The production brigade is a political and
economic unit in rural China which ranks just below the commune.
On the average each brigade includes 1,000 people or 200 families.
The brigade will often administer a primary school and medical sta-
tion. It plays an intermediate role in negotiating agricultural
production and delivery plans between teams and higher
authorities.

Production Team. The production team generally has fifty families or 100–250 people and is based on a small hamlet of a neighborhood within a larger village. Team leaders make the day-to-day decisions on farming and record the team members' work points which determine individual shares of the team income.

Work Points. Members of production teams are assigned work points according to the particular tasks they perform. Work points are totaled up by the team accountant and are used to determine the shares of the collective income paid to each family. The value of each work point is based on the total team income divided by the total number of work points earned by all members.

Marriage Law of 1980. The Marriage Law of 1980 was essentially a continuation of the Marriage Law of 1950, which granted freedom of choice in marriage, granted women the right to divorce, outlawed the selling of brides, and banned many traditional marriage customs that discriminated against women. The Marriage Law of 1980 raised the legal age for marriage from 18 to 20 for females and from 20 to 22 for males. It also further liberalized divorce procedures and stated that children had the legal obligation to provide for their parents in old age.

Cultural Revolution. See Part One.

Review Questions

1. In what ways was the Chinese family viewed as the key to a good society, according to Whyte's introductory essay?

2. According to Whyte, what has been the attitude of the government toward the family since 1949?

3. What is the hierarchy or order of priority within lineages and families, according to "Family Instructions"?

4. As presented in "Family Instructions," what are the special responsibilities of parents? Of youngsters?

5. In the excerpt from Ba Jin's book *The Family*, what were Chueh-hsin's own aspirations, and why was he unable to realize them?

6. What was Chueh-hsin's attitude toward the frustrations of his own goals, and how did he resolve this conflict in his life?

7. According to the article by Wang and Li, what are the causes of the high expenditure of time spent on housework in contemporary urban China?

8. What are the effects of the burdens of housework on the individual? On society?

9. According to Mary Sheridan's article, what were the limitations on Xiuyin's life because of the "feudal" attitudes of her family and her husband?

10. How did life in Xiuyin's village change for women after Liberation?

11. According to Emily Honig's article in the Reader, what political factors were involved in Yu Luojin's two marriages?

12. What were the differing points of view about "mutual affection" or love in marriage that were debated in Yu Luojin's second divorce case? What was her "radical definition"?

13. According to the video "Marrying," what are some of the major differences in attitudes toward women and marriage between traditional China and the official policies of China today?

14. What elements of the traditional wedding ceremony do the couple in "Marrying" retain? What are government policies toward such traditions today? Why does the couple nevertheless opt for these traditions?

UNIT SIX: CREATING A BROADER COMMUNITY

Study Components

Video: "Caring"

The Heart of the Dragon, by Alasdair Clayre: Chapter Four, "Mediating," pp. 91–104

Readings from *The Chinese*: Introduction to Part Three and Chapter Six, "Creating a Broader Community"

1. "Urban Social Control," by Sybille van der Sprenkel

2. "The Commune as a Social System," by Martin K. Whyte

3. "A Chinese Hospital," by Gail E. Henderson and Myron S. Cohen

4. "My Neighborhood," by B. Michael Frolic

5. "Connections," by Zheng Yefu

Learning Objectives

To become acquainted with:

— traditional and modern forms of community and grass roots organizations

— the importance of the work-unit (*danwei*) in Chinese society

— the traditional and renewed use of personal "connection" (*guanxi*) networks

— the structure and function of neighborhood committees in urban China

— the organization of health care and social welfare services

Overview

Although Chinese families and kin groups sometimes act as if they were islands unto themselves, cooperation outside of the family has nonetheless been important. To illustrate China's heritage of social organization, this unit begins with Sybille van der Sprenkel's discussion of two types of unofficial organizations, guilds and temple associations, during the Qing dynasty (1644–1911). Such unofficial organizations, which arose among common interest groups, coexisted with a territorial network of official, centralized organizations for exercising imperial authority. Temple associations were responsible for the maintenance of local temples, but they also served political, economic, and social functions. The fact that members shared religious beliefs enforced the authority of their leadership and provided a basis for resolving disputes among members. Guilds were largely responsible for the economic activities of townspeople, including establishing standards appropriate to their businesses and adjudicating disputes among members. The state could intervene in the economy, but detailed regulation was usually left to the guilds. Van der Sprenkel's article thus highlights the importance in traditional China of group solidarity and the interplay between official and unofficial social organization.

Rural areas had similar systems of local organization, including self-help and religious groups, as Martin K. Whyte points out in his introduction to Part Three. The Chinese Communist revolution was based in the countryside, and it was rural China that experienced the most sweeping changes after 1949. The program of land reform begun in Communist base areas prior to 1949 ultimately led to the elimination of the small but powerful landlord class that had previously controlled rural society. In his selection in the Reader, "The Commune as a Social System," Whyte sketches the development of the new system of rural administration after 1949. During the early 1950s the government began to encourage the consolidation of individual landholdings into ever larger cooperatives that were designed to pool tools and animals and regulate labor exchanges. The form of rural organization—communes, brigades, and production teams—that eventually took shape has been in place since 1962. Formally the structure has remained essentially the same, but significant policy changes have occurred in recent years. In an effort to spur agricultural production, the state has granted production teams more autonomy, employed economic incentives, expanded free markets, and contracted private plots to individual families. These changes are discussed in more detail in Part Four, Chapter Eight.

Contemporary social organization in urban China is examined in the article by Gail Henderson and Myron Cohen, who lived for six months in a provincial hospital. This selection examines the role of the work-unit (*danwei*) of a Chinese hospital. In the early 1950s the government restricted migration to urban areas and centralized control over job and housing assignments. All workplaces in urban China were organized into administrative units. Each urban worker is assigned to a work unit that serves social, political, and economic functions. Although each work unit is under the jurisdiction of a higher bureaucractic unit, each remains relatively isolated and contact between units can be problematic.

Another form of urban organization is described in B. Michael Frolic's article on neighborhood committees, which demonstrates how effective the extension of official government organization to the grass roots levels has been in China. The neighborhood committee is an arm of higher level political control, but it is also a means by which a community administers itself. In many ways it is similar to the unofficial organizations described by van der Sprenkel. Unlike traditional forms of local control, however, it is more tightly linked to the state, and each committee includes a member of the Public Security Bureau, although the neighborhood committee is staffed almost entirely by local residents. It is clear from this article, as well as from the video "Caring," how essential this form of social organization is to the maintenance of order and community well-being in China's cities.

Zheng Yefu's essay introduces us to the importance of "connections" (*guanxi*) in Chinese society. The use of connections—based on family ties, school ties, common geographic origin, or other particularistic ties—has a long history in China. According to Zheng, this reliance on connections is a part of the undesirable residue of China's past, whose abuse has been exacerbated by economic shortages and a loss of spiritual morality brought about by the Cultural Revolution. Zheng proposes the establishment of a rational legal system coupled with a renewal of spiritual morality as a solution to the reliance on connections. The continual shortages of adequate housing and the limited availablity of medical and some consumer goods, however, provide the type of environment in which the reliance on connections seems unavoidable. Rejecting Western materialism, he urges a new morality that will maintain the

Chinese feeling for human relationships and create a modern, distinctively Chinese ethic and social order.

The video "Caring" provides a look at modern China's urban social organization, focusing on a Chinese prison, a hospital, and a mental hospital. Continuing themes are evident: orientation toward the group rather than the individual, respect for order, and trust in authority. These are particularly clear in both the prison and mental hospital, where there is a strikingly similar emphasis on reforming incorrect attitudes, thoughts, and behavior. The workings of the neighborhood committee depicted in the video are nearly identical to those described in B. Michael Frolic's article and in Chapter Four of *The Heart of the Dragon*. Alasdair Clayre observes that elderly women constitute a majority on most neighborhood committees and seem to have assumed the moral authority that matriarchs once had in traditional extended Chinese families. The continued importance of the family and the group as opposed to the individual are also discussed by Clayre in Chapter Four and repeatedly illustrated in the video. As in the past, neighborhoods continue to share a group responsibility for local order. This has been a hallmark of Chinese society but, as the narrator comments, it often comes at the expense of personal initiative and individuality.

Key Concepts

Danwei. In the early 1950s all workplaces in urban China were organized into *danwei* or administrative units. Each urban worker is assigned to a work unit that serves social, political, and economic functions. The unit assigns housing and access to social services and is also the center for discussion of local and national concerns.

Neighborhood Committees. The neighborhood committee is an arm of higher level political control but it is also a means by which a community administers itself. Most of the members are local residents, usually retired women, though each committee includes a member of the Public Security Bureau. Neighborhood committees settle local disputes, monitor neighborhood security, maintain buildings, and provide information on public health and birth control.

Responsibility System. A major feature of the recent economic reforms, the responsibility system, has replaced collectivized farming in the countryside. Under this system individual households contract land from the state and assume the responsibility to supply a specified amount of their output, at fixed prices, to the state. Surplus production remains under the control of the individual family and can be sold on the free market. In the past all land was farmed collectively and the surplus was divided among members of production teams. Current reforms call for a responsibility system in industry as well. Workers would be responsible for a specified amount of production and would be rewarded with bonuses for surplus production. Failure to fulfill quotas would also be grounds for dismissal.

Iron Rice Bowl. Traditionally, the Chinese referred to their means of earning a livelihood as a "rice bowl." Under today's socialist system, the "iron rice bowl," which cannot be broken, serves as a metaphor for total job security.

Guanxi. The Chinese term *guanxi* literally means "relationships," but in the present context it is better translated as "connections." The use of personal connections, such as family ties, school ties, and common place of origin, to obtain favors, bureaucratic advancement, or cement political ties has a long history in China.

Review Questions

1. What kind of rural social organization existed in traditional China, according to Whyte's introductory essay in the Reader?

2. What were some of the flaws in the social reforms of "the new order"?

3. What were the two traditional kinds of social control, as described by van der Sprenkel in her article in the Reader on nineteenth-century imperial China?

4. What were two traditional types of social groups described by van der Sprenkel, and how did these associations provide order and community in towns?

5. Describe the basic functions of each administrative level of the commune system, as discussed by Whyte in the Reader.

6. What are the different methods by which income was distributed in the commune system, according to Whyte?

7. What is a *danwei*, and what traditional social, political, and economic functions does it have, as described by Henderson and Cohen in the Reader?

8. What factors other than the *danwei* affect the lives of the members?

9. What are the structure and functions of the residents' committee, as described in "My Neighborhood" in the Reader?

10. What opinions did the neighborhood committee member form about urban community organization in China, as compared to that in Hong Kong?

11. What are *guanxi*, and why were they so integral a part of traditional Chinese society? What does Zheng Yefu mean by a "personalized ethic"?

12. What factors does Zheng Yefu cite for the reemergence of "connections," and what suggestions does he make for eliminating reliance on them?

13. What are some of the basic, and distinctively Chinese, attitudes toward children, old people, community, medicine, mental health, and treatment of criminals, as portrayed in the video "Caring"? How do these contrast with Western attitudes?

14. How have social changes affected traditional Chinese family and community life, as seen in the video "Caring"? What is the interplay between official and traditional means of "caring"?

15. What major reason is given in the video for the current problem of disaffected youth?

UNIT SEVEN: CLEAVAGES AND SOCIAL CONFLICTS

Study Components

Video: "Mediating"

The Heart of the Dragon, by Alasdair Clayre: Chapter Four, "Mediating," pp. 104–8

Readings from *The Chinese:* Introduction to Part Three and Chapter Seven, "Cleavages and Social Conflicts"

1. "Subethnic Rivalry," by Harry J. Lamley

2. "The Position of Peasants," by Sulamith Heins Potter

3. "The Class System of Rural China," by Jonathan Unger

4. "Birth Control: A Grim Game of Numbers," by Steven W. Mosher

5. "Rural Violence in Socialist China," by Elizabeth Perry

Learning Objectives

To become acquainted with:

— some sources of social conflict in imperial China

— the restrictions and disabilities associated with peasant status

— social discord caused by the use of "class labels"

— problems associated with enforcement of birth control policies

— the reappearance of social conflict resulting from reforms of rural organizations

— the role of mediation committees in divorce and other social problems

Overview

Respect for authority and the maintenance of social harmony have always been highly valued in China. Nevertheless, as in other societies, ethnic and religious differences in China have sometimes been sources of social cleavages and violence. Lamley's reading discusses the violence between subethnic groups in Taiwan during the eighteenth century, when Taiwan was still a frontier area. Many of the settlers came from areas in the southeast where subethnic differences, in this case primariliy Hokkien and Hakka groups, had long been a source of violence. Within each rival group common geographic origin, family and clan ties, and ethnic background provided cohesion. Violence was frequently highly organized and took place on such a large scale that government intervention was required to restore peace.

Another important cleavage within Chinese society occurs between urban and rural households. Sulamith Heins Potter's essay on the position of peasants describes the disadvantages and limitations of rural residency. Under the Household Registration Act of 1959, residency status is ascribed at birth, thus effectively prohibiting migration to urban areas. Despite decades of Maoist praise of peasant life, the preference for urban living is apparent both in the urban resident's dread of being sent down to the countryside and in the peasant's envy of the comforts and opportunities of urban life.

According to the *Communist Manifesto*, written by Karl Marx and Friedrich Engels, "The history of all hitherto existing society is the history of class struggle." The concept of class struggle and a class-based analysis of society were two elements of Marxist ideology basic to Mao's thought. Unlike Western Marxists, however, Mao believed that class conflict could continue after the establishment of socialism. Jonathan Unger describes the application and consequences of the use of class labels in post-1949 China in association with land reform policies and the effort to dismantle the traditional socioeconomic structure of Chinese society. Discrimination based on bad class background was common in the past, but the present leadership has repudiated this aspect of Maoist thought.

The urgency and potential excesses of China's drive to control population by stringent measures limiting family size are evident in the reading by Steven Mosher. As his account demonstrates, recent government intrusions into family life can be traumatic and sometimes result in violence. The strength of traditional values regarding family and children, discussed in Chapter Four of *The Heart of the Dragon*, present a formidable obstacle to the one-child policy. This problem is particularly severe in rural China, where the absence of social security for the aged, along with opportunities created by the new reforms, add an economic incentive for having large families.

The video "Mediating" further illustrates some of the problems associated with the one-child birth control policy, which range from divorce to female infanticide. As the video illustrates, when the dictates of policy confront traditional values the consequences can be disastrous. The social pressure to conform that local mediation committees bring to bear can be overwhelming and—as the reconciliation in the video seems to show—effective.

Although recent reforms have led to increased productivity and higher standards of living, this very success has also had some unintended repercussions. Elizabeth Perry, whose article appears in the Reader, has carefully pieced together scattered reports of recent incidents of social conflict in rural China. The adoption of the responsibility system, whereby individual families have become self-employed, has led to a disparity in incomes and greater competition for resources between rival units. Resentment toward the newly rich has occasionally erupted into violence. In some cases these incidents resemble the feuding based on local and clan ties described by Lamley. The reappearance of secret societies centered on popular religions has also caused alarm among China's leaders. This is especially true when rural cadres, whose positions have been undermined by the new economic freedoms, have been involved. Communist Party officials increasingly find themselves treading a treacherous path between the need for economic reforms and the unforeseen consequences of their policies.

Key Concepts

Household Registration System. Under the Household Registration
Act of 1959, residency—either urban or rural—is ascribed at birth.
Peasants are designated as rural personnel, which means that they
are not eligible to take jobs or live in urban areas. In his article in
the Reader Jonathan Unger refers to this situtation as birth-
ascribed stratification.

State's Rice. This term is used by Chinese peasants in reference to
the food available to urban workers. Unlike peasants who grow
their own grain, urban workers purchase rice from the state at sub-
sidized prices.

Going Down to the Countryside. During the Cultural Revolution
many intellectuals, party members (including Deng Xiaoping), and
urban youth were sent down to the countryside to perform manual
labor, in what amounted to a program of labor reform. Ostensibly,
this policy was designed to bridge the gap between urban and rural
China, but more often it was considered a form of punishment.
Despite efforts to correct it, some victims of this policy are still
unable to reestablish their urban residency.

Class Labels. In the early 1950s each household in China was
ascribed a class label based on its socioeconomic status. Members
of revolutionary classes, such as peasants and workers, received
good class labels, while former capitalists or landlords were considered bad class elements. Such labels were particularly important
during the process of land reform. For example, households designated as landlord class had much of their land confiscated. These
class labels became fixed so that future generations continued to
bear the stigma of a bad class label regardless of their current
socioeconomic status.

One-child Policy. In an effort to limit population growth, the
Chinese government has adopted a policy of one-child-per-family.
Under this policy families who agree to the one-child limit are
rewarded with a variety of benefits, such as better access to health
care and educational facilities. Similarly, there are penalties for
families who exceed the one child limit. To date the policy has been

successful in urban areas, but it has met resistance in the countryside where there are economic advantages to larger families.

Native Place Associations. During imperial times native place associations were present in most large Chinese cities. These associations were usually organized according to provincial origin and they served as meeting places and hostels for travelers, usually merchants.

Guilds. Guilds were a form of urban social organization made up of persons engaged in the same business or craft. The primary function of guilds was to establish local control over a profession or craft by setting standards of workmanship and price, protecting the business from competition, and settling disputes among guild members.

Liberal and Statist Options. During the Republican period (1912–49) Chinese intellectuals and politicians offered a variety of visions of China's future. Martin Whyte, in his introductory essay, refers to these as the "liberal" and "statist" options. According to Whyte, the liberal option advocated the development of a modern state machinery, a well-developed legal system, an extensive marketing system, and the freeing of individuals from the excessive demands of and loyalties to their families and other social groups. The "statist" option advocated many of the same goals but its distinctive feature was the belief that individual freedom from group constraints was very dangerous, with chaos the likely result. The proper solution was not to free individuals from the demands of families and personalistic groups, but to change the nature of these groups so that they would work to the benefit of society. It should be noted that advocates of the liberal option were largely intellectuals with little, if any, political power.

Review Questions

1. What might be some of the undesirable consequences of the post-Mao reforms, according to Whyte's introductory essay in the Reader?

2. As discussed in the Lamley article in the Reader, what factors determined the composition of the subcultural feuding groups in Taiwan during the Qing (Ch'ing)

period, and what organizations were the focus of these
groups?

3. What political-economic reasons does Lamley give for
   the factional disputes?

4. What were the historical circumstances for the es-
   tablishment of the "Regulations for Household
   Registration," as given in the Potter article in the
   Reader?

5. How did the regulations affect peasants as compared to
   workers? What effects did the regulations have on the
   relations between the two groups?

6. What reasons are given in the Unger article in the
   Reader for the system of class labels established in the
   early 1950s?

7. Why were class label policies discarded after Mao's
   death?

8. As recounted in the Mosher article in the Reader, what
   arguments did the cadres use to get women to "think
   clear" about abortions? What methods of persuasion
   did they use?

9. According to Perry's article in the Reader, what
   aspects of rural organization have spurred the reemergence of intensified parochial loyalties and rural
   violence?

10. What reasons does Perry suggest for the revival of
    traditional religious practices, and what is their role in
    rural violence?

11. As revealed in the video "Mediating," why have
    Chinese families traditionally wanted a large number of
    children, and especially sons?

12. Why is the population control issue so important to the
    state?

13. What methods and appeals do the mediators use in the case illustrated in the video? How does the Chinese attitude toward this family rift and potential divorce differ from Western attitudes?

PART THREE:
ESSAY/DISCUSSION QUESTIONS

1. Discuss traditional attitudes toward the individual in the Chinese family, and the extent to which these attitudes have—or have not—changed in contemporary China.

Suggested Guidelines:

a. Consider the role of the family and its hierarchy, referring especially to:

- the introduction to Part Three in the Reader

- *The Heart of the Dragon* (pages 68–69)

- the selections by Ebrey, Ba Jin, and Sheridan in the Reader

- the function of the matchmaker in the video "Marrying"

b. Refer to the role of the government since 1949 as discussed in:

- the introduction to Part Three of the Reader

- *The Heart of the Dragon* (pages 80–82)

- Honig's essay in the Reader, especially concerning policies during the Cultural Revolution and the divorce debate

- Sheridan's account of the role of the village production team, in the Reader

- the videos "Marrying" and "Mediating" concerning population control

c. Contrast the marriage situations of Chueh-hsin in Ba Jin's story and Yu Luojin in Honig's essay, both in the Reader, and compare each of them with that of the couple in the videos.

d. Consider the relationship between men and women, referring to:

- the housework burden in the study by Wang Yalin and Li Jinrong in the Reader

- Sheridan's account in Zhao Xiuyin's marriage, in the Reader

- the definition of the basis of marriage by Yu Luojin's opponents in Honig's essay in the Reader

- the couple in the videos "Marrying" and "Mediating"

- the discussion throughout the chapter "Marrying" in *The Heart of the Dragon*

2. How has community organization since 1949 changed from imperial times? Consider both rural and urban areas, and both Maoist and post-Mao eras.

Suggested Guidelines:

a. Consider the traditional roles of government, family, and the social network, referring to:

- van der Sprenkel's discussion of imperial control and urban groups, and Zheng Yefu's discussion of "connections," both in the Reader

- Clayre's chapter "Mediating" in *The Heart of the Dragon* (pages 91–93), discussing family and social order

- the introduction to Part Three in the Reader on the subject of non-family groups and social networks

- Lamley's discussion of subethnic groups, also in the Reader

b. Consider the effects of the reforms since 1949? Refer to:

- the introduction to Part Three in the Reader, discussing the aims and dilemmas of the state under and after Mao

- the Whyte article on communes and the Sheridan article "Lady of the Sties," both in the Reader, with attention to the relation of the family unit to socialist rural organization and the factors affecting the solidarity of the rural social system

- "The Chinese Hospital" in the Reader, concerning the functions and organization of the *danwei*

- the Frolic selection in the Reader, and the role of the residents' committees

- Zheng Yefu's discussion in the Reader of the increased reliance on "connections"

- *The Heart of the Dragon* (pages 93–102), concerning Communist Party social policies

- the videos "Caring" and "Mediating" on the relationships among family, individuals, and the state

3. What cleavages in China's social order have been generated as a result of changing Communist Party policies?

Suggested Guidelines:

a. Consider policies that have directly affected families and individuals, referring to:

- the video "Mediating" and the Mosher article in the Reader, comparing traditional attitudes toward family size and current state problems and policies regarding population

- the introduction to Part Three of the Reader concerning the effect of post-Mao economic reforms on decisions among individuals and neighbors

b. Consider how state policies have affected relations between subgroups, and between classes. Refer to:

- the Potter article in the Reader; what does "eat the state's rice" mean, and what does the phrase reflect about the effect of the classification system on social cohesion?

- the Lamley and Potter articles in the Reader, concerning tension between traditional rural subgroups

- Unger's article in the Reader and his suggestion of why and how authorities have encouraged "scapegoating"

c. Consider how official policies have affected people's attitudes toward the state, referring to:

- the introduction to Part Three in the Reader concerning expectations since the Revolution, and to Clayre's discussion of order, family, and Party policies in the chapter "Mediating" in *The Heart of the Dragon*

- Maoist and post-Maoist policies, as discussed in the introduction to Part Three in the Reader. How do they compare?

- Perry's description in the Reader of the factors affecting the revival of traditional religious practices

Part Four
The Economy

Part Four introduces us to the economy of China, focusing on agriculture, industry, and trade in imperial and Communist China. This section of the course highlights the methods, progress, and remaining problems of China's drive to modernize its economy.

UNIT EIGHT: AGRICULTURE

Study Components

Video: "Living"

The Heart of the Dragon, by Alasdair Clayre: Chapter Six, "Living"

Readings from *The Chinese:* Introduction to Part Four and Chapter Eight, "Agriculture"

1. "The Chinese Peasant Economy," by Ramon H. Myers

2. "Marketing and Social Structure in Rural China," by G. William Skinner

3. "The Commune System Before Reform," by Frederick W. Crook

4. "Socialist Agriculture Is Dead; Long Live Socialist Agriculture!" by Kathleen Hartford

Learning Objectives

To become acquainted with:

— peasant life in China, past and present

— the economic and political organization of rural China

— the marketing and social structure of rural China

— the effects and possible implications of economic reforms
   in the countryside

— the responsibility system and its impact on the rural
   economy

— the present state and future requirements of agricultural
   technology

Overview

   The video "Living" and Chapter Six of *The Heart of the Dragon*
both introduce us to the Chinese peasantry, who make up 80 per-
cent of the Chinese population. Centuries of hard work have altered
the landscape of China, enabling Chinese agriculture to support an
ever-growing population. In some ways the life of the peasant has
changed very little, since Chinese agriculture today remains highly
labor-intensive and much of the work done still relies on human
labor. The similarity between the Yuan dynasty (1269–1368) painting of peasants at work on page 133 of *The Heart of the Dragon* and
the contemporary photo on page 143 provides a striking illustration
of this continuity. Nevertheless, changes have occurred in the
economic and social organization of the rural sector. Peasants have
benefited from increased access to education, medical care, and
rural electrification. In contrast to the past, the government has
played a much more active role in organizing peasants to build the
rural infrastructure and to increase productivity. During the 1950s
these efforts were sometimes counterproductive, but under the current responsibility system productivity has increased and living

standards have risen. As in the past, the family has reemerged as the basic economic unit.

The Reader selection by Ramon Myers is based on village studies carried out by the Japanese during their occupation of North China in the 1930s. The deterioration of the rural economy and the breakdown of rural society during the twentieth century, and its political implications, have been the subject of much debate among China scholars. Myers' examination of the data for several villages in North China finds that the effects of economic depression and war were variable. Throughout this period agricultural productivity kept pace with population growth, and peasant households, which remained the basic economic and social unit, responded rationally to changing economic circumstances. According to Myers, the government's failure to provide adequate education and support for technological development was the major impediment to further economic growth. In contrast to Myers, who emphasized technological development and lack of government support, some specialists have argued that the commercialization of Chinese agriculture, a process exacerbated by imperialism, sharply skewed the distribution of wealth and engendered increased conflict between landowners and peasants.

Skinner's article provides a perspective on the agricultural marketing system. Skinner applies the principles of central place theory, combined with his own fieldwork in Sichuan, to uncover the limitations the marketing structure imposed on the development of Chinese agriculture. According to his findings, the high cost of transportation and transaction costs limited the size of the market system, thus restricting the development of Chinese agriculture.

As mentioned in earlier units of this course, after 1949 a revolutionary program of land reform was implemented and China's agricultural sector underwent extensive institutional reorganization. This was the most immediate and far-reaching result of the Communist revolution. The commune structure of political and economic organization that emerged is the subject of the reading by Frederick Crook. The overall results were favorable, but at times the penetration of the government into rural society meant misguided and harmful interference in agriculture. He notes that artificial administrative boundaries, the centralization of administrative and economic decision making, and the lack of economic incentives limited agricultural productivity.

In 1978 institutional organizations were reformed once again to grant greater freedom to individual families. Hartford's article out-

lines the benefits of the new organizational reforms but emphasizes
the need for technological inputs. In a sharp departure from Maoist
models, peasants now contract land from the state and are essentially self-employed. Under this system peasants have prospered.
Autonomy is limited, however, and peasants are still obligated to
sell a portion of their produce to the state. Similarly, the peasant
must still rely on the state to provide investment capital for the new
technology that is necessary if agricultural productivity is to continue to increase.

Key Concepts

*Technologist and Distributionalist Explanations of Constraints on
Agriculture.* Western scholars have offered many different explanations of why China's agricultural economy failed to achieve a successful transition to the high yields of modern scientific agriculture.
Ramon Myers' selection in the Reader is an example of the technologist argument which blames the failure of the government or
educational system to make modern technology available to the
peasants. Distributionalists argue that commercialization of
agriculture in the twentieth century led to a worsening of income
distribution between owners of land and tillers of land. According to
this explanation, those who had the capital to invest in technology
were using these funds for investment in other sectors or for the
consumption of luxuries, while the poorer peasants lacked the
means to invest in modern technology.

Production Responsibility System. The production responsiblity system for agriculture was first introduced in 1978. Although its form
may vary, it has retained two common features: production contracts between production teams and smaller units below the
teams—usually households—and differential compensation distin-
guishing the work contribution of each producer. In most cases individual households contract land from the state. Production teams
retain a role in centralized production planning, but day-to-day
management devolves to individual households.

Specialized Household. The contracting of land to individual
households has led to a more efficient use of labor, which in turn
has produced a surplus labor force in the countryside. To remedy
this problem rural cadres have arranged contracts with peasants

whose special productive skills require little or no land, such as bee-keeping or livestock-raising, or individuals may enter small-scale production, repair work, or commerce using their own investment funds. Such households are known as specialized households.

Review Questions

1. According to Dernberger's introduction to Part Four of the Reader, what is the nature, and what are the causes, of China's current population problem?

2. What features of China's traditional economic system accounted for the success of Chinese agriculture in the eighteenth and nineteenth centuries, according to Dernberger?

3. In Myers' study of the traditional system of private farming in the Reader, what economic factors do all the villages have in common?

4. What reasons does Myers give for the maintenance of living standards despite population increases? What inputs does he cite as necessary to improve agricultural production?

5. What is the spatial model of the hierarchical system of the traditional market structure, as described by Skinner in the Reader?

6. What are the functions of the standard and intermediate markets, respectively? How do they eventually form a society-wide economy?

7. According to the Crook article in the Reader, how did the aims of the commune system reflect Mao's vision of a socialist society? How was the system organized to implement Party aims in both economic goals and political behavior?

8. What is Crook's assessment of the strengths and weaknesses of the commune system?

9. What are the basic mechanisms of the responsibility system discussed in the Hartford article in the Reader?

10. How, in Hartford's view, does the emerging new model for Chinese agricultural production retain the same root assumptions as the Maoist model?

11. What difficulties does Hartford see for the agricultural reforms? What does she think is necessary for China to break through its "developmental impasse" in agriculture?

12. As presented in the video "Living," what changes in official attitude are reflected in the new responsibility system? How has this organizational innovation affected the villagers of Maoping?

13. What factors give the life of China's "farm people" such stability, as seen in the video "Living"? What worries China's leaders about recent economic gains?

14. As presented in the video, what are the duties of Mr. Fang, the Communist Party secretary in Maoping?

UNIT NINE: INDUSTRY

Study Components

Video: "Working"

The Heart of the Dragon, by Alasdair Clayre: Chapter Seven, "Working"

Readings from *The Chinese:* Introduction to Part Four and Chapter Nine, "Industry"

1. "The Foreign Establishment in China in the Early Twentieth Century," by Albert Feuerwerker

2. "China's Transition to Industrialism," by Thomas G. Rawski

3. "China: The Economic System," report by the World Bank

4. "The Chinese Economy: The Awakened Dragon?" by Robert F. Dernberger

Learning Objectives

To become acquainted with:

— the foreign economic presence in China during the twentieth century

— the impact of foreign enterprises on indigenous industrialization

— economic, especially industrial, development during the first half of the twentieth century

— the essential features of the Soviet economic model

— the scope of recent economic reforms in China

— the work environment and quality of life of the Chinese worker

Overview

Industrialization is a recent phenomenon in China that began only after the country was opened to foreign trade in the nineteenth century. Marxist historians in China argue that there were indications of indigenous capitalism in late imperial China that were snuffed out by the intrusion of the imperialist powers. Throughout the nineteenth century foreign powers pressured the imperial government to open an increasing number of cities to foreign trade (see Chapter Ten of the Reader for details). Within these cities, known as treaty ports, foreign businessmen were immune from

Chinese law and enjoyed other privileges such as low or flat customs duties. The humiliating manner in which China was opened to foreign trade during the period from 1840 to 1949 has left a bitter residue in the minds of many Chinese. While Western economists may approach the problem of China's early industrialization from a purely economic standpoint, for the Chinese it is often a deeply emotional issue involving national pride.

Chinese nationalists from both ends of the political spectrum have argued that the failure of China's early efforts to industrialize was due largely to the privileged status of foreign enterprises. One fact is clear: prior to 1949 foreign enterprises dominated China's modern industrial sector. The impact of the foreign economic presence in China is the subject of a balanced essay by Albert Feuerwerker, which is sensitive to both the economic and political dimensions of this question. In his systematic examination of trade, banking, manufacturing and mining, transport, and public finance, he concludes that foreign economic gains were not an absolute deduction from China's economic welfare and that the pyschological and political impact of the foreign presence had a far more significant effect on the course of China's modern history.

During the first half of the twentieth century, political turmoil, foreign competition, and war limited the growth of native Chinese industry. Nevertheless, Thomas Rawski's research reveals that during this period Chinese entrepreneurs and engineers developed skills that provided a base for industrial expansion after 1949. His study focuses on engineering firms, originally established to repair and service foreign machinery, and on the entrepreneurial skills that the Chinese learned from their foreign competitors. Thus, despite the apparent weakness of Chinese industry prior to 1949, significant gains were being made in several important areas. Rawski's essay is representative of the more detached, strictly economic evaluations of China's early industrialization.

After 1949 China turned to the Soviet Union for economic assistance and guidance. The locomotive factory featured in the video "Working" is just one example of Soviet economic aid. China's Communist leaders also adopted the Soviet economic model, which is the subject of the World Bank study included in the readings. Under this highly centralized system, the Communist Party determines economic policy and the state manages the national economy; market forces have virtually no impact on economic decisions. Annual plans, based on administrative decisions, determine the flow of resources, prices, wages, and labor-power allocation. As we learn in the video, inefficiencies have plagued the system. In an attempt to resolve this problem, recently implemented policies aim at decentralizing control and making enterprises responsible for profits and losses.

The video "Working" and the Chapter "Working" in *The Heart of the Dragon* also introduce us to industrial life in China. The workers portrayed occupy a key economic and political position in Communist society, and the Chinese state is very sensitive to their needs and attitudes. Industrial jobs are highly prized, since they offer lifetime security and a wide range of social services. Yet the hazardous working conditions, long hours, and party control depicted in the video reveal that the material rewards and political status of workers have their price. The future also poses questions for workers, as the new responsibility system threatens to shatter the "iron rice bowls" of unproductive workers.

China's leaders have recently announced a wide range of economic reforms, but it remains to be seen how thoroughly these reforms will be implemented. Robert Dernberger's article assesses the impact of those reforms that actuallly have been put into practice. These reforms—which include reduction of central planning, more autonomy for individual factory managers, creation of private and collective enterprises to compete with state-owned enterprises, relaxation of state control over the allocation of the output of goods and services, and price reform—lead in the direction of what Dernberger calls a "mixed economic system." Difficulties have been experienced with each of these reforms, and the present state of the reform program thus appears to be more of a case of "muddling through" rather than a coordinated program. But, according to Dernberger, these reforms represent a considerable improvement over the economic situation of the last decade.

Key Concepts

State Enterprises. State owned and administered enterprises dominate the Chinese economy. The state appoints the management personnel, decides annual production targets, and determines wages and prices. There are also a small number of private enterprises, including self-employment and workers collectives, that are nominally owned by their members. Unlike state enterprises which remit profits directly to the state, collectives pay taxes on their profits, but for most practical purposes collectives are indistinguishable from state-owned enterprises.

Soviet-style Economic System. Under Stalin's leadership, in the 1920s and 1930s the Soviet Union developed economic policies and institutions designed to secure industrial development. The Soviet experience later became a model for other Communist countries. The Soviet model is characterized by the mobilization of a high rate of savings for the purpose of investing in production facilities for the heavy industrial sector. Resources and commodities are allocated according to plans and administrative directives implemented by a centralized bureaucracy.

Market Socialism. Market socialism is a term used to describe a socialist economy in which market forces, the law of supply and demand, play some role in the allocation of resources and commodities. The extent to which market forces are a factor may vary and, in the case of China, recent reforms have lead to a relaxation of some features of the Soviet-style economic model described above. Nevertheless. the state still retains ownership of the means of production and control over the distribution of most resources.

Review Questions

1. According to Dernberger's introduction to Part Four in the Reader, what factors inhibited the development of industry in China?

2. In what ways did the Chinese reorganize China's industrial sector after 1949, according to Dernberger's introduction?

3. According to Feuerwerker's selection in the Reader, what were the political, economic, and psychological effects of the foreign presence in China?

4. In Feuerwerker's view, what were the factors responsible for China's slow economic growth?

5. In Rawski's selection in the Reader, how does he account for the growth of Chinese industries before 1937,

which, in his view, laid a foundation for continuing development in the producer sector?

6. As documented in the World Bank study in the Reader, what are the basic instruments of management of China's socialist economic system?

7. According the the World Bank report, how are jobs allocated in the Chinese economic system? What methods are used to remunerate workers in state organizations and urban collectives, including items of income support?

8. What is the relationship of China's domestic and export prices to the world market, as discussed in the World Bank report?

9. What are the major aims of the Eight Character Program, formally adopted in 1979, as outlined by Dernberger in the Reader?

10. According to Dernberger, how is the center of gravity of China's economic activities shifting? What are the three factors that the author sees as producing a "mixed system" of economic management?

11. What are the advantages and disadvantages of being an industrial worker in China, as revealed in the video "Working"?

12. How has the introduction of the responsibility system affected workers, as shown in the video "Working"? What problems are being addressed by the state with this system?

UNIT TEN: TRADE

Study Components

Video: "Trading"

The Heart of the Dragon, by Alasdair Clayre: Chapter Eleven, "Trading"

Readings from *The Chinese:* Introduction to Part Four and Chapter Ten, "Trade"

1. "Foreign Trade and Industrial Development of China," by Yu-kwei Cheng

2. "China's Balance of Payments in the Twentieth Century," by Nai-ruenn Chen

3. "Economic Modernization in Contemporary China: Limiting Dependence on Foreign Technology," by Robert F. Dernberger

4. "China's Economy and Foreign Trade, 1981–85," by Nai-ruenn Chen and Jeffrey Lee

Learning Objectives

To become acquainted with:

— the conduct of foreign trade in traditional China

— the opening of China to foreign trade during the nineteenth century

— the unequal treaties and the development of the treaty port system

— the influence of politics on foreign trade policy after 1949

— current reforms in the conduct of foreign trade

— the establishment of special economic zones

Overview

The Chinese have never looked upon foreign trade as simply an economic matter. Since the early days of the Silk Road, pictured in the video "Trading," Chinese emperors sought strict control over the conduct of foreign trade. Trade was often conducted under the guise of tribute missions to the emperor. Regardless of the actual circumstances, Chinese emperors welcomed foreign merchants as emissaries of foreign rulers wishing to bestow gifts in recognition of the supreme position of China's emperor. There were also more practical political reasons for closely monitoring foreign trade. Quite frequently such foreign ideas as Islam and Buddhism were imported along with foreign goods. Similarly, the imperial state recognized the potential political threat of a wealthy merchant class. Merchants were relegated to the lowest social status in imperial China, beneath scholars, peasants, and artisans.

For centuries the Chinese were able to exercise some degree of control over the flow of foreign trade, but this situation changed dramatically in the nineteenth century when China was confronted by the militant economic power of the West. Yu-kwei Cheng's article traces the evolution of the treaty port system that was imposed on China over the course of the nineteenth century. Prior to the Opium War in 1842, trade with the West was restricted to the southern port of Guangzhou (Canton). The Treaty of Nanjing, signed by China after its defeat by Britain, opened the way to greater foreign penetration of the Chinese economy and new concessions from the feeble imperial government. By the turn of the century the imperialist powers had divided China into exclusive spheres of influence, causing many observers to fear that Chinese sovereignty would be extinguished completely. Resentment of imperialism fed nascent Chinese nationalism and gave birth to a broad range of political movements which eventually combined to overthrow the imperial government in the Revolution of 1911.

Throughout the first half of the twentieth century China suffered from a large foreign trade deficit. Some scholars have argued that this deficit drained the Chinese economy of the capital needed for economic modernization. Nai-ruenn Chen's essay argues that the remittances from overseas Chinese laborers, businessmen, and entrepreneurs financed this deficit. Over time, he argues, the Chinese economy benefited from being able to import more commodities than were being exported. Chen, like Rawski, adopts a purely economic calculus to examine what is for the Chinese also an emotional and political issue. Although his argument may be sound economically, it is important to realize that very few Chinese at the time perceived the problem in these terms. Many Chinese continue to harbor bitter memories of the one-hundred-year history of imperialism in China and this sentiment still influences contemporary debates over increasing foreign trade.

Since 1949 the Chinese attitude toward foreign trade has sometimes appeared contradictory. Economic policy has alternated between periods of self-reliance and periods of active borrowing of foreign technology. According to Robert Dernberger, this issue became a major point of contention among China's leaders, and the dramatic shifts in political power over the last thirty-five years are reflected in China's foreign trade patterns. In addition, he argues that an awareness of modern technology's potential to undermine political and social institutions, as it did in the late nineteenth century, has militated against a more open trade policy. The current regime is therefore concerned to limit the impact of China's opening to the outside world. As we see in the video "Trading," one solution has been to limit foreign investment to special economic zones. Ironically, the most important of these zones is located not far from Guangzhou, where the foreign penetration of the Chinese economy began in the nineteenth century.

Despite the cautious trade policies of the past, the emphasis on self-reliance has been eclipsed and China's present leadership appears determined to proceed with the large-scale acquisition of technology from the industralized countries of the West. The article by Jeffrey Lee and Nai-ruenn Chen summarizes the reforms in this area and points out some potential problems. Continued expansion of foreign trade will require loans to finance imports and investment, but so far China's leaders have been reluctant to incur a large foreign debt. Import restrictions in foreign markets may also limit the extent of China's foreign trade. Until these issues are resolved, the possibility of a return to the policy of self-reliance cannot be ruled out.

Key Concepts

Treaty Ports. Prior to the Opium War in 1842, foreign trade with China was limited to the southern port of Guangzhou (Canton) and the right to trade with foreigners was limited to licensed Chinese merchants known collectively as the *Co-Hong.* After the signing of the Treaty of Nanjing, the number of ports opened to foreign trade gradually increased. Since foreign trade was restricted to ports opened by treaty, they became known as treaty ports. The "most-favored-nation" provision soon became a feature of all commercial treaties concluded between China and the foreign powers. The most-favored-nation provision meant that whenever China granted additional rights and privileges to a foreign power, all other nations with most favored nation status automatically received the same rights and privileges. In contrast to the present day usage of the most-favored-nation provision, however, foreign powers did not grant similar status to China.

Spheres of Influence. During the late nineteenth century, imperialist powers in China attempted to extend their economic rights and privileges in China through the establishment of spheres of influence. Unlike the colonial situation in Africa and other parts of Asia, although the imperialist powers exerted political and economic influence within their spheres of influence, actual political administration remained in Chinese control. These spheres of influence included: the British in the Yangzi valley, the French in south and southwest China, the Russians in northern Manchuria, the Germans in Shandong province, and the Japanese in southern Manchuria.

Open Door Policy. The meaning of the "open door policy" in China has changed since it was first proposed by the United States in the early twentieth century. At that time the United States feared that the creation of exclusive spheres of influence by the imperialist powers in China would undermine Chinese sovereignty and lead to exclusion of American products from the China market. Thus, the United States proposed an Open Door Policy that called for respect of Chinese sovereignty and equal economic opportunity for all foreign powers in China. At the time, the proposal received little support from the foreign powers and many Chinese politicians denounced this policy as a justification for even greater foreign

penetration of China's economy. Currently, the term open door
policy is used by the Chinese themselves to describe the reopening
of China to foreign trade, in contrast to the "closed door" or autarkic
policies of the Maoist era.

Autarky. Autarky is the policy of establishing a completely self-
sufficient national economy independent of imports from other
countries. While autarky was a cornerstone of Maoist economic
policy begining in the late 1950s, the cutoff of Soviet aid in 1960
(economic aid from the Soviet Union was an important component
in Chinese economic development after 1949) and the United States
trade embargo of China that began in 1949 (see Chapter Ten of *The
Heart of the Dragon*) left the Chinese little alternative but to pursue
an autarkic policy. Since the normalization of relations between the
United States and China and the abandonment of Maoist economic
policies, foreign trade has grow rapidly as the Chinese seek foreign
technology to aid in their modernization program.

Technological Imperative. Some social scientists have argued that
modern technology determines certain policies and patterns of behavior. This process is known as the technological imperative.
Technology that was developed in the West in a particular institutional environment might thus generate forces that undermine
the institutions of a different environment or culture into which the
technology is transferred. According to Robert Dernberger's selection in the Reader, the Maoist emphasis on economic self-reliance
was based partly on an awareness of this problem.

Special Economic Zones. In the post-Mao era of economic reform,
the Chinese have established a series of special economic zones to
attract foreign investors. Within these zones special tax incentives
and preferential treatment with regard to land, raw materials, customs regulations, labor contracts, and foreign currency controls are
granted to foreign investors. The major zones are located in the
south near Hong Kong and in Fujian. Ordinary Chinese are not allowed access to these zones, thus limiting the impact of the foreign
presence on the Chinese society and economy.

Review Questions

1. As discussed in the Yu-kwei Cheng article in the Reader, what were the reasons for the Opium War, and what were its effects on China's relations with foreign powers?

2. What factors does Yu-kwei Cheng cite as having hampered the development of China's foreign trade?

3. What factors does Nai-ruenn Chen cite in his article in the Reader as being responsible for the growth of Chinese imports, slow export growth, and the long-term deficit?

4. How, according to Nai-ruenn Chen, was China able to finance the persistent trade deficit from the end of the nineteenth century to 1940?

5. In what way does Yu-kwei Cheng disagree with Nai-ruenn Chen's thesis that China's passive trade balance was counterbalanced by foreign investments?

6. According to Dernberger's selection in the Reader, what has been the ambivalence in China's attitude toward economic relations with foreigners?

7. How did Mao view the problems generated by the importation of foreign technology? What advice did Mao give and how, in Dernberger's view, has Mao's advice succeeded?

8. From Nai-ruenn Chen and Jeffrey Lee's article in the Reader, what are China's current economic aims and foreign trade priorities?

9. How do Nai-ruenn Chen and Jeffrey Lee detail China's efforts to balance centralization and decentralization regarding foreign trade policy? What do they see as the problems of centralization?

10. What balances and unknowns do Nai-ruenn Chen and Jeffrey Lee see as important to the future of China's foreign trade?

11. As shown in the video "Trading," what were the effects on China of its early history of foreign trade?

12. How did the Cultural Revolution affect China's entrepreneurs, as shown in the video "Trading"? How have attitudes and policies changed since then, and for what reasons?

13. How have new policies affected social habits, especially in urban areas, according to the video? Do you think fear of Westernization is well-founded?

PART FOUR:
ESSAY/DISCUSSION QUESTIONS

1. What major problems have the different Communist systems of agricultural organization tried to solve? And how does the new responsibility system relate to the traditional system of agricultural production?

Suggested Guidelines:

a. Review Clayre's chapter "Living" (pages 141 ff) in *The Heart of the Dragon*, concerning the various Communist policies.

b. Consider the constraints on development in the agricultural sector, referring to:

   • the headnote to the Skinner article in the Reader describing the "technologist" and "distributionalist" explanation for slow growth

   • the Hartford and Myers' articles in the Reader regarding the need for improved technology

- the Skinner discussion in the Reader of traditional village-regional marketing structures, and the Hartford suggestion, also in the Reader, of a contradiction between comparative regional advantages and central planning

- the Crook and Hartford discussions, in the Reader, concerning motivational factors and income distribution; also discussed in the video "Living"

- Hartford's forecast of difficulties in the new model of socialist agriculture

c. Consider the similarities and differences between the traditional system and the responsibility system, with reference to:

- Hartford's new model of socialist agriculture, as compared with Myers' description of traditional village organization (both in the Reader), with attention to responsibilities for decisions affecting uses of land, labor, production, distribution, compensation, and labor-intensive organization

- the video "Living" and the interplay between tradition and change

2. How have the Chinese Communists dealt with the need for modernization in the industrial sector of their economy?

Suggested Guidelines:

a. Consider the state of the industrial sector they inherited, referring to:

- Feuerwerker and Rawksi, both in the Reader, and their arguments concerning the impact of the foreign presence on the economy

- the introduction to Part Four in the Reader, and the discussion of China's industrial revolution

b. Review the Soviet model discussed in the headnote to the World Bank study and in the study itself, with attention to:

- tiered governmental structure

- enterprise plans and targets

- methods of determining money and commodity flows, and price controls

c. Refer to Clayre's discussion in "Working" in *The Heart of the Dragon*, regarding:

- the importance of heavy industry to China's growth

- the various plans, from the first Five Year Plan on, and the problems encountered

d. Consider the state's problems as seen in the video "Working," and its methods of dealing with them, with special attention to:

- motivation and training

- the conflict between full-employment policies and the need for greater efficiency

- the impact of the responsibility system

e. Consider Dernberger's analysis of the post-Mao reforms in Chapter Nine of the Reader, especially in the areas of:

- the aims of the reforms

- the relationship among state, collective, and individually-operated enterprises

- the contrast between guidance and mandatory planning

- the allocation of goods and services

- price determination and the relationship between centralized planning and market forces

3. What are the reasons for China's somewhat ambivalent attitude toward opening the country to foreign trade, and what effect has this ambivalence had on policy since 1949?

Suggested Guidelines:

a. Consider the history of China's trade relations, referring to:

- Murphey's introduction to Part One of the Reader and the documents in Chapter One

- Yu-kwei Cheng's discussion in Chapter Ten of the Reader, especially about the century of imperialism and China's efforts to restrict foreign trade

- Clayre's historical review in the chapter "Trading" in *The Heart of the Dragon*

- the video "Trading" concerning foreign influences and Chinese attitudes toward foreigners historically

- Nai-ruenn Chen's article in the Reader on the influences of the foreign powers on China's trade deficit from 1898 to 1940

- Yu-kwei Cheng and Nai-ruenn Chen's articles in Chapter Ten of the Reader and the articles by Feuerwerker and Rawski in Chapter Nine. Consider their different views of the economic effects of the foreign presence

b. How have the conflicting attitudes been reflected in
   radical shifts in the pattern of China's foreign trade?
   Refer to:

   ● Dernberger's discussion in the Reader of policy
     shifts, Mao and post-Mao attitudes toward the "tech-
     nological imperative," and a policy of dual technologi-
     cal development (capital-intensive and labor-
     intensive)

   ● Clayre's review in "Trading" in *The Heart of the
     Dragon* of the Mao and post-Mao policies

c. Consider current policies, referring to:

   ● Nai-ruenn Chen and Jeffrey Lee's discussion in the
     Reader of China's current aims, incentives for
     foreign economic activity, and attempts to constrain
     foreign influence.

   ● the video "Trading," showing current attitudes
     toward Chinese capitalists and private enterprise,
     free markets, overseas Chinese, joint ventures, and
     concerns about the effects of foreign influence on
     Chinese culture and society

Part Five
Culture

Part Five introduces two aspects of culture which, in traditional China, were highly integrated: literature and the arts, and science and technology. This section of the course focuses on trends in Chinese culture and on the relationship of the arts and of science and technology to the political and economic goals of China.

UNIT ELEVEN: LITERATURE AND THE ARTS

Study Components

Video: "Creating"

The Heart of the Dragon, by Alasdair Clayre: Chapter Ten, "Creating"

Readings from *The Chinese:* Introduction to Part Five and Chapter Eleven, "Literature and the Arts"

1. "K'ung I-chi," by Lu Hsün (Lu Xun)

2. "Talks at the Yan'an Conference on Literature and Art," by Mao Zedong

3. "The Wounded," by Lu Xinhua

4. *"Death of a Salesman* In Beijing," by Yuan Henian

5. "A Misty Manifesto," by Hong Huang and "Three Poems," by Bei Dao

Learning Objectives

To become acquainted with:

— a broad survey of Chinese art and literature

— traditional Chinese approaches to art

— some themes in modern Chinese fiction

— the Maoist interpretation of the relationship between literature and the arts and revolution

— the impact of the Cultural Revolution on contemporary artists and writers

Overview

Four thousand years of Chinese civilization have yielded a rich tapestry of literature and art. Chapter Ten of *The Heart of the Dragon* presents various examples of Chinese literature and art from the past to the present and discusses the philosophical and cosmological understandings that have informed the arts in China. As the video "Creating" illustrates through the work and reflections of artists in different disciplines, Chinese artists have always been mindful of the work of their predecessors; the resonances of the past continue to inform and guide the literature and art of the present. Despite greater openness to foreign influences, the arts in China retain qualities which are uniquely Chinese.

Chinese intellectuals and artists have always occupied an important and influential place in society. For this reason literature and art have often been subjected to careful scrutiny by China's rulers. Nowhere has the relationship between culture and politics been more clearly enunciated than in Mao Zedong's "Talks at the Yan'an Conference on Literature and Art." Mao's message was clear: literature and art must serve the revolution. He urged artists and writers to learn from the masses and to produce a new literature and art that derived its content from popular life.

In the course of his talks, Mao praised Lu Xun (Lu Hsün), regarded as one of modern China's greatest writers of fiction. Lu was a member of the vanguard of Chinese writers who called for an abandonment of elite literary styles and the use of a vernacular style that could reach a wider audience. The sample of his work included in these readings is a satire of traditional intellectuals, designed to point out the weaknesses of traditional culture.

In the video "Creating" we meet several artists and writers who were victims of the Cultural Revolution. Traditionally, Chinese writers and artists have believed that their work should express their unalterable inner convictions. Thus the Cultural Revolution was particularly difficult for them and today they are beginning to express the sufferings of this period in their work. Lu Xinhua's story is an example of the "Literature of the Wounded," stories of the emotional and personal consequences of the Cultural Revolution.

The basic tensions that underlie China's struggle to modernize — including the ambivalence toward foreign influences — are apparent in contemporary literature and art. In recent years there have been numerous indications that the government has become more tolerant toward the arts. In 1983 the Beijing People's Art Theatre staged a production of *Death of a Salesman* under the direction of Arthur Miller. Cultural exchanges and opportunities for Chinese artists and writers to study abroad have also increased. The "Misty Manifesto" by Hong Huang and the poetry of Bei Dao appear to herald new vistas in both content and form in Chinese literature. If the political climate remains unchanged, Chinese literature and art may be entering a new and richer stage of development.

Key Concepts

Qi. *Qi*, alternately translated as "configured energy" and "energetic configurations," is a vitalizing energy that is both universal and highly particular. *Qi* plays an important part in Chinese cosmological and metaphysical thought. At times it means the spirit of life in living creatures; at other times it is the air or ether surrounding the universe. In some contexts it denotes the basic substance of all creation.

May Fourth Movement. See Unit One.

The Literature of the Wounded. The Literature of the Wounded is the work of a new generation of Chinese writers who came of age during the Cultural Revolution. Severely critical of the Gang of

Four, their novels and stories represent a rigorous self-examination of the people who were caught up in the excesses of the Cultural Revolution. This body of work has been promoted by China's leaders, many of whom also suffered during the Cultural Revolution.

Misty Poetry. Misty Poetry is also called the "New Poetry of the New Chinese Generation." It is a movement dedicated to forging a new poetry free of the formal and contextual restraints of traditional Chinese poetry, as well as contemporary ideological restraints. Simultaneously, it also seeks a return to the ambiguity, nuance, and striking imagery of traditional work.

Review Questions

1. According to DeWoskin's introduction to Part Five in the Reader, what constitutes the traditional concept of "culture" in China?

2. What was the role of literature and the arts in traditional Chinese society?

3. In the story "Kung I-chi" in the Reader, what is the author's attitude toward China's traditional culture, and how is this conveyed?

4. What did Mao claim, in his speech at the Yan'an Conference included in the Reader, to be the source of literature and art and the relationship of literature and art to politics?

5. What were Mao's stated attitudes toward ancient and foreign literature and art, and toward the individual artist?

6. Why do you think "The Wounded," included in the Reader, has been considered a "flagship piece" of post-Cultural Revolution literature?

7. What seem to be the strengths and weaknesses of life in a collective, as depicted in "The Wounded"? What

contradiction in Maoist thought, as presented in the story, affects Xiaohua's life?

8. Why was the play *The Death of a Salesman* considered an especially appropriate choice for presentation in China?

9. How do the content and form of the "new poetry," as discussed in "A Misty Manifesto" in the Reader, differ from both traditional and revolutionary poetry?

10. What aspects of the new poetry do Bei Dao's poems reveal?

11. As shown in the video "Creating," what Chinese religious and philosophic concepts have been important in Chinese arts? How does the Chinese view of "reality" compare with Western views?

12. As portrayed in the video "Creating," what has been the effect of Communist ideology in general, and of the Cultural Revolution in particular, on attitudes toward, and experiences of, artists in China? How have these conflicted with traditional attitudes?

UNIT TWELVE: SCIENCE AND TECHNOLOGY

Study Components

Video: "Understanding"

The Heart of the Dragon, by Alasdair Clayre: Chapter Nine, "Understanding"

Readings from *The Chinese:* Introduction to Part Five and Chapter Twelve, "Science and Technology"

1. "Chinese Science: Explorations of an Ancient Tradition," by Nathan Sivin

2. "Science in Contemporary China," by Leo A. Orleans

3. "National Plan for the Development of Science and Technology (1975–85)," by Fang Yi

4. "Electronics," by Bohdan O. Szuprowicz

Learning Objectives

To become acquainted with:

— the historic contributions of Chinese science and technology

— several hypotheses to explain the arrested development of science in China

— the major branches of scientific study in traditional China

— the concepts of *yin* and *yang* in medicine and science

— the development of science in China since 1949

— the future goals of scientific and technological development in China

Overview

Given the current state of Chinese scientific and technological development, it is easy to forget that as late as the seventeenth century Chinese science was unsurpassed by that of any other civilization. After all, the compass, gunpowder, paper, and printing were all invented in China. In the chapter "Understanding" in *The Heart of the Dragon*, Alasdair Clayre offers several interesting hypotheses to explain why Chinese science failed to fulfill its early promise. Nathan Sivin's article in the Reader delineates the basic categories of early Chinese science: medicine, alchemy, astrology, geomancy, physical studies, and mathematics. He also makes the point that cultural perceptions have a great impact on scientific thought.

One fundamental principle of early Chinese science was the belief that the natural world was governed by a balance of opposing forces called *yin* and *yang*. The Chinese believed that all changes occurring in nature were a result of the interplay of these two forces. The video "Understanding" and Chapter Nine of *The Heart of the Dragon* present several examples of how this principle was applied to medicine, astrology, and physical studies. The application of this principle in the practice of medicine continues to this day.

The video "Understanding" also shows a stunning example of how seismology has benefited from the blending of traditional and modern technology. Indeed, much of Chinese science has benefited from the longstanding Chinese respect for knowledge and scholarship. As discussed in the Reader selection by Leo Orleans, which deals with post-1949 scientific development, Mao himself was a strong advocate of modern scientific research (although he also urged Chinese scientists to learn from the past). The Great Leap Forward and the Cultural Revolution slowed advances in scientific knowledge, however, and the closing of universities during the Cultural Revolution left a serious generation gap within the scientific community. To remedy this situation the state has invested more heavily in scientific development and provided more opportunities for scientists to study abroad. By promoting scientific research, China's leaders hope to increase economic output, upgrade national defense, and garner greater international recognition and prestige.

Thus, under the program of the Four Modernizations, the modernization of science has been designated as the key link which will propel advances in agriculture, industry, and national defense. As Fang Yi, former Minister of the State Science and Technology Commission, points out in his speech excerpted in the Reader, China urgently needs to improve virtually every area of scientific and technological study. The objectives spelled out in Fang's speech are ambitious and, some would say, represent a wish list more than a practical program for development. Nevertheless, some significant gains have already been made. As we see in the video "Understanding," Chinese laser technology has advanced markedly in just a few years.

Szuprowicz's article in the Reader charts Chinese advances since 1949 in another field: electronics. While he identifies many areas requiring further work, he also notes that the Chinese have made considerable progress despite political disruptions, low levels of investment, and a weak technological base.

Yet another area in which Chinese science has had marked success is in medicine. As seen in the video "Understanding," in 1965 Chinese scientists were the first to produce synthetic insulin. With greater investment in research and increased contacts with the international scientific community, the prospects for scientific and technological advance appear quite good.

Key Concepts

Mutation Theory. In mutation theory, qualitative changes in physical states are related to numerological structures such as hexagrams, as in the *Yijing* [I-ching], or *Book of Changes*, explaining how the elements of the Five Phases (see below) produced each other.

Resonance Theory. Resonance theory is a Daoist concept which explains causation in nature. Daoists believe that the symbolic correlations in all things form one colossal pattern. Things behave in certain ways because their position in the ever-moving cyclical universe endow them with an intrinsic nature which make their behavior inevitable. Things in the universe which belong to the same class (see the Five Phases below) resonate with, or energize, each other.

Yin-Yang. *Yin* and *yang* described perfect opposition within a perfect unity. Anything at any time at any place has a *yin-yang* relationship with some other thing, time, or place. Female is *yin* to male as *yang*. The moon is *yin* to the sun as *yang*. North is *yin* to south as *yang*. This concept of two primal forces or modes of creation first became a major element of Chinese thought during the Han dynasty (202 B.C.–220 A.D.).

Alchemy. Alchemy is a chemical science and speculative philosophy that aims to achieve the transmutation of the base metals into gold, the discovery of a universal cure for disease, and the discovery of a means of prolonging life indefinitely. Alchemy was an important component of Daoism.

Geomancy. Geomancy is a branch of traditional Chinese science that is used to determine the auspicious placement of houses and tombs with respect to features of the landscape.

Five Phases. The Five Phases—wood, fire, metal, water, and earth—are similar in concept to the *yin-yang* theory. Like *yin* and *yang*, the phases are metaphysical forces or modes which dominate or control certain periods of time, commonly the seasons, in a fixed succession. Wood is assigned to the season of spring; fire to summer; metal to autumn; and water to winter. Since there are only four seasons, earth, associated with the color yellow, is commonly assigned a position in the center, aiding the other elements in their governing of the four seasons.

Review Questions

1. What factors retarded the growth of Chinese science in the first half of the twentieth century, according to DeWoskin's introduction to Part Five of the Reader?

2. As discussed in the Sivin article in the Reader, what were the most common tools of abstract thought in ancient China? What basic understanding of nature did they convey?

3. Give examples of how these traditional "tools" and their underlying concepts affected some of the major scientific disciplines.

4. According to the article by Orleans in the Reader, what have been China's development priorities since 1949? What does the author conclude are China's two most pressing problems in connection with modernization?

5. What factors does Orleans cite as having impeded China's modernization? How does his explanation compare with DeWoskin's and Clayre's?

6. What advantages to the United States and other developed nations can cooperation with Chinese scientists provide, according to Orleans?

7. In Fang Yi's speech in the Reader, what were the modernization aims articulated by Chairman Mao and Premier Zhou? What eight spheres does Fang Yi list

as most important to the Eight Year Plan for modernizing science and technology?

8. What organizational changes does Fang Yi outline for implementing the policy goals?

9. Why are electronics and computer technology so important to China, as discussed in the Szuprowicz article in the Reader?

10. What is the status of China's computer industry today, according to Szuprowicz?

11. As shown in the video "Understanding," what is the Chinese understanding of the heavens, earth, and humans? What basic concepts express these views?

12. What were some of the major Chinese inventions and discoveries in science, as shown in the video? What were the impediments to China's continued advance in this area?

PART FIVE:
ESSAY/DISCUSSION QUESTIONS

1. Discuss the changing attitudes toward and roles of the arts in China in this century.

Suggested Guidelines:

a. Consider the traditional attitudes and roles, referring to:

- DeWoskin's discussion of the role of the arts in imperial China, in the introduction to Part Five of the Reader

- the video "Creating" and Clayre's chapter "Creating" in *The Heart of the Dragon* concerning the influence of Daoism, Buddhism, and Confucianism

- the discussion in the video on different art forms

- Clayre's discussion of the aims of traditional painting in the chapter "Creating" in *The Heart of the
  Dragon*, especially concerning the concept of *qi* and
  the northern and southern schools of landscape
  painting

b. Review the reform movements, with reference to:

- the introduction to Part Five in the Reader about the
  May Fourth Movement and to "Kung I-chi" concerning the Movement's attitude toward tradition and literary reform

- Mao's attitude toward tradition and foreign influence, expressed in "Talks at the Yan'an Conference" in the Reader

- "A Misty Manifesto" and attitudes toward both
  traditional and revolutionary poetry

- the video "Creating," showing the attitudes of artists
  concerning Western art and its relation to Chinese
  art forms.

c. Consider the experiences of artists during the Mao and
   post-Mao years, as revealed in:

- the video "Creating," especially the relationship between artists and politics

- Mao's attitudes toward artists

- the story "The Wounded" in the Reader, and the conflict between individual feelings and loyalties, and
  political dictates

- the review of *Death of a Salesman* in the Reader and
  Chinese interest in both indigenous values and
  Western life

2. What is the traditional Chinese understanding of the relationship between the body and the universe, and how has this shaped traditional medicine in China?

Suggested Guidelines:

a. Review the traditional concepts and their applications in Clayre's chapter "Understanding" in *The Heart of the Dragon*, the video "Understanding," and the introduction to Part Five and Sivin's article in the Reader, with attention to:

   ● the concepts of *qi* and *yin/yang*

   ● the understandings of illness and health

   ● the attitude toward the earth (refer also to Murphey's "Man and Nature in China" in Chapter Two of the Reader)

   ● the relationships among the body, mind, and nature

3. In his selection in the Reader, Orleans says "The PRC is by no means a typical developing country." Discuss the meaning of this quote with reference to China's history of scientific achievements, the reasons for a decline, and the goals of and obstacles to current policies.

Suggested Guidelines:

a. Consider China's long history of discovery and invention, and the reasons for the decline in science, referring to:

   ● Clayre's chapter "Understanding" in *The Heart of the Dragon* and the video "Understanding"

   ● DeWoskin's discussion in the introduction to Part Five of the Reader

b. Review China's current priorities in science and technology, referring to the articles by Orleans, Fang Yi,
   and Szuprowicz in the Reader

c. Consider the enormity of the challenge of scientific
   modernization, with reference to the impediments to be
   overcome, as discussed in :

   - the introduction to Part Five in the Reader, especial-
     ly regarding ambivalent attitudes toward foreign in-
     volvement

   - the Orleans and Szuprowicz selections in the Reader
     on the effects of the Cultural Revolution

   - Fang Yi's speech in the Reader, and the implications
     of deficiencies in institutional structures

Part Six
The Future

Part Six speculates on likely future developments in China, considering economic, political, and social problems as well as Sino-American relations.

UNIT THIRTEEN: CHINA'S PROSPECTS

Study Components

Readings from *The Chinese*: Introduction to Part Six and Chapter Thirteen, "China's Prospects"

1. "Economic Marathon," by Robert Delfs

2. "Jiangsu Villagers Show Off the Future," by Dai Yannian

3. "'A Fly in a Bottle,' That's Me," by Zhang Xinxin and Sang Ye

4. "Chinese Democracy and Western Values," by Andrew J. Nathan

5. "The United States' Interest in China," by Michel Oksenberg

Learning Objectives

To become acquainted with:

— China's economic goals for the year 2000

— likely changes in rural life-styles

— some negative aspects and potential problems of the current reform program

— political reforms at the grass roots level

— current state of Sino-American relations and propects for the future

Overview

Throughout this course we have looked at the influence of China's past on its recent, ongoing struggle to modernize. While innovation in political, social, and economic institutions are altering the face of contemporary China, many traditional values and beliefs continue to shape Chinese attitudes and behavior. The readings in Chapter Thirteen look at China's prospects for the future. In the past, Western observers have not had much success in predicting China's future. For example, the Cultural Revolution, which had such an enormous impact on Chinese society, took most outside observers by surprise. Thus, while all predictions of China's future remain tentative at best, this chapter provides some educated guesses as to what the future might hold for China.

Economic growth and improvements in living standards are a top priority for China's current leaders. Robert Delfs' article supplies a summary of a World Bank study of the Chinese economy and plans for its future development. On the basis of past performance, the prospects for economic growth seem bright; however, as this report cautions, present targets may be too ambitious. Aside from purely economic considerations, popular reaction to economic reform is an important but less tangible element, which cannot be ignored. As the report notes, price reforms are badly needed, but it is feared that increased prices could trigger panic buying and infla-

tion. Similarly, the report suggests that under the new responsibility system, a commodities future market will be needed to
protect farmers from price volatilities and to induce investment in
agriculture. Such commodities trading, however, is a form of
speculation that is currently illegal in China. Future economic goals
have been highly publicized and consequently have produced high
expectations among the people. Should the Chinese economy falter,
the political repercussions could be serious.

To date the greatest improvements in living standards have occurred in the countryside. Dai Yannian's report on Ouqiao village
in Jiangsu presents an idealized picture of what the future holds for
China's peasants, noting gains in cultural as well as material life.
There is no mention of the types of problems we read about in
Chapter Seven. Not everyone has prospered under the new reforms
but, according to Dai, successful peasants have not neglected less
fortunate villagers. In contrast to this optimistic account, however,
recent press reports have also noted tensions resulting from growing disparities in income and local government exploitation of the
newly rich.

"'A Fly in a Bottle,' That's Me" provides a glimpse at the
downside of the new reforms. Luo Bin, an unemployed youth, expresses bitterness toward those who have profited from reform and
and from the use of "connections," which have been more fully
described in Chapter Six of the Reader. As we learned in the video
"Working," underemployment has been a serious problem in China
for some time. Economic expansion may eventually provide some
relief, but in the meantime resentment among the unemployed
grows. At times this resentment has been vented against the special treatment accorded foreigners, who are given access to the best
hotels and restaurants and to special stores which stock higher
quality merchandise. Such favoritism toward foreigners is designed
in part to attract foreign tourists with their foreign exchange; it also
makes life more comfortable for the growing number of foreign ex-
perts and teachers who are needed in China's drive toward modernization. These practices also make it easier for Chinese authorities
to monitor the activities of foreigners and to limit their contact with
the Chinese people. Oddly enough, despite his misgivings Luo still
professes support for communism and the leadership of Deng Xiaoping.

Some Western observers have speculated that economic reforms
in China will also lead to greater demands for political reforms and
a more democratic form of government. Andrew Nathan's article

examines both the recent political reforms and the concept of political participation in China. Although the present political system does allow for greater popular participation, he concludes that the average citizen remains more an object of control rather than an exerciser of influence. While the form of pluralistic democracy practiced in the West is not without its advocates in China, the fledgling democracy movement that appeared in 1979 has been effectively crushed.

The prospects for future cooperation between the United States and China are examined in the essay by Michel Oksenberg who, as a member of the National Security Council during the Carter administration, played an active role in normalizing Sino-American relations. He calls for a clear statement of U.S. expectations of China and he cites a broad range of common interests which bode well for future cooperation. He also identifies some potential areas of conflict, but notes that for the time being, potentially disruptive issues such as the resolution of the Taiwan question have taken a backseat to economic and scientific cooperation. It remains to be seen if the good will built up during this period of cooperation will pave the way for a long-standing partnership between the world's largest developing country and the world's largest developed country.

Review Questions

1. According to Goldstein's introduction to Part Six, what are the three most likely scenarios for China's future?

2. What is China's long-term economic aim, its interim plan to reach that goal, and the World Bank's assessment of the primary factor affecting the goal, as suggested in the Reader?

3. How does the World Bank's "balance scenario" present an alternative to China's stretegy, and what are the major areas of economic reform discussed in the report?

4. How have reforms benefited the Jiangsu village described in the Reader? Which sector of the village economy has contributed most to the increased

prosperity, and how has it affected other aspects of village life?

5. In "'A Fly in a Bottle,' That's Me," in the Reader, what is the youth's attitude toward the recent changes in China? Why does he call himself a "fly in a bottle"?

6. What is the Chinese government's theory of democracy, as discussed in the Nathan article in the Reader, and how do the recent political reforms relate to that theory?

7. What is the difference between the Chinese Communist definition of democracy and a Western, pluralist definition?

8. As described by Nathan, what have been the goals of the Chinese democrats, and what has been their reception by the government and by most intellectuals?

9. In Nathan's view, what questions are there concerning the feasibility of pluralist democracy in China?

10. What long-term considerations does Oksenberg cite in his article in the Reader as underlying improved Sino-American relations?

11. What "pitfalls" does Oksenberg see in "Chinese futurology," and what new priorities in Sino-American relations does he recommend?

PART SIX:
ESSAY/DISCUSSION QUESTION

1. How do the authors of this final chapter evaluate the future of China's reform movement?

Suggested Guidelines:

a. Review the changes and problems of the "More Likely Futures" discussed in the introduction to Part Six in the Reader.

b. Consider the challenges still confronting China's economy, referring to the World Bank study in the Reader, with attention to:

   • the economic-management system

   • decentralization

   • expansion of international contact, and the benefits and risks of foreign trade and investment

   • investment "hunger"

   • the credit system

c. Compare the Jiangsu villagers' attitudes with those of the urban youth in "'A Fly in a Bottle,' That's Me." both in the Reader. Consider the differential economic impact and new social tensions generated by new policies. (Refer also to Chapter Seven, "Cleavages and Social Conflicts," in the Reader.)

d. Consider Oksenberg's discussion of the need for new priorities in Sino-American relations that have emerged as the reforms have opened China to the international community and strengthened China's economic and technological development. What are these recommended new objectives and areas of concern, and why does he conclude that American and Chinese strategic and economic interests are basically congruent?

APPENDICES

1. MAPS AND OTHER AIDS

Maps

Illustrated Atlas of China. Chicago: Rand McNally Co., 1972.
The Times Atlas of China. New York: New York Times Book Col, 1974.

Reference Works

Bartke, Wolfgang. *Who's Who in the People's Republic of China.* Armonk, New York: M.E. Sharpe, 1981.
Dillon, Michael. *Dictionary of Chinese History.* London: Frank Cass and Company, 1979.
Hook, Brian, general editor. *The Cambridge Encyclopedia of China.* London: Cambridge University Press, 1982.
Mackerras, Colin. *Modern China: A Chronology from 1842 to the Present.* London: Thames & Hudson, 1982.

Periodicals and Newspapers

Beijing Review. A weekly magazine published in English which includes both domestic and international news.
China Daily. An eight page English-language newspaper published in Beijing. Subscriptions can be obtained from: *China Daily* Distribution Corp., 15 Mercer Street, Suite 401, New York, NY 10013.

China Reconstructs. A monthly magazine published in English with color photographs, which includes feature stories on economic development, tourism, the arts, medicine, and national minorities.

Information on subscriptions and on other English-language materials published in China can be obtained from: China Books and Periodicals, 2929 24th Street, San Francisco, CA 94110.

2. PINYIN PRONUNCIATION GUIDE

The *pinyin* system of romanization, adopted in the People's Republic of China after 1949, has increasingly replaced the older Wade-Giles system in contemporary Western writings on China. As noted in the textbook, *The Chinese*, the editors have used *pinyin* in both their introductory essays and the headnotes that precede the various readings. The following pronunciation guide and *pinyin/*Wade-Giles conversion chart are provided to help familiarize the non-specialist with these romanization systems.

Pinyin is pronounced phonetically, except for:

c: sounds like the *ts* in *its*
e: sounds like the second *a* in *gallant*
e: when directly before *ng*, *e* sounds like the *u* in *hung*
o: sounds like the *aw* in *saw*
ou: sounds like the *o* in *slow*
q: sounds like the *ch* in *China*
x: sounds like the *sh* in *shell*
zh: sounds like the *j* in *junk*

3. PINYIN/WADE-GILES CONVERSION CHART

Pinyin	Wade-Giles		Pinyin	Wade-Giles
a	a		cen	ts'en
ai	ai		ceng	ts'eng
an	an		cha	ch'a
ang	ang		chai	ch'ai
ao	ao		chan	ch'an
ba	pa		chang	ch'ang
bai	pai		chao	ch'ao
ban	pan		che	ch'e
bang	pang		chen	ch'en
bao	pao		cheng	ch'eng
bei	pei		chi	ch'ih
ben	pen		chong	ch'ung
beng	peng		chou	ch'ou
bi	pi		chu	ch'u
bian	pien		chuai	ch'uai
biao	piao		chuan	ch'uan
bie	pieh		chuang	ch'uang
bin	pin		chui	ch'ui
bing	ping		chun	ch'un
bo	po		chuo	ch'o
bou	pou		ci	tz'u
bu	pu		cong	ts'ung
ca	ts'a		cou	ts'ou
cai	ts'ai		cu	ts'u
can	ts'an		cuan	ts'uan
cang	ts'ang		cui	ts'ui
cao	ts'ao		cun	ts'un
ce	ts'e		cuo	ts'o

Pinyin	Wade-Giles		Pinyin	Wade-Giles
da	ta		ge	ke, ko
dai	tai		gei	kei
dan	tan		gen	ken
dang	tang		geng	keng
dao	tao		gong	kung
de	te		gou	kou
dei	tei		gu	ku
di	ti		gua	kua
dian	tien		guai	kuai
diao	tiao		guan	kuan
die	tieh		guang	kuang
ding	ting		gui	kuei
diu	tiu		gun	kun
dong	tung		guo	kuo
dou	tou		ha	ha
du	tu		hai	hai
duan	tuan		han	han
dui	tui		hang	hang
dun	tun		hao	hao
duo	to		he	he, ho
e	e, o		hei	hei
ei	ei		hen	hen
en	en		heng	heng
eng	eng		hong	hung
er	erh		hou	hou
fa	fa		hu	hu
fan	fan		hua	hua
fang	fang		huai	huai
fei	fei		huan	huan
fen	fen		huang	huang
feng	feng		hui	hui
fo	fo		hun	hun
fou	fou		huo	huo
fu	fu		ji	chi
ga	ka		jia	chia
gai	kai		jian	chien
gan	kan		jiang	chiang
gao	kao		jiao	chiao

Pinyin	Wade-Giles	Pinyin	Wade-Giles
jie	chieh	liao	liao
jin	chin	lie	lieh
jing	ching	lin	lin
jiong	chiung	ling	ling
jiu	chiu	liu	liu
ju	chü	long	lung
juan	chüan	lou	lou
jue	chüeh	lu	lu
jun	chün	luan	luan
ka	k'a	lun	lun
kai	k'ai	luo	lo
kan	k'an	lü	lü
kao	k'ao	lüe	lüeh
ke	k'e, k'o	ma	ma
ken	k'en	mai	mai
keng	k'eng	man	man
kong	k'ung	mang	mang
kou	k'ou	mao	mao
ku	k'u	mei	mei
kua	k'ua	men	men
kuai	k'uai	meng	meng
kuan	k'uan	mi	mi
kuang	k'uang	mian	mien
kui	k'uei	miao	miao
kun	k'un	mie	mieh
kuo	k'uo	min	min
la	la	ming	ming
lai	lai	miu	miu
lan	lan	mo	mo
lang	lang	mou	mou
lao	lao	mu	mu
le	le	na	na
lei	lei	nai	nai
leng	leng	nan	nan
li	li	nang	nang
lia	lia	nao	nao
lian	lien	ne	ne
liang	liang	nei	nei

Pinyin	Wade-Giles	Pinyin	Wade-Giles
nen	nen	qiao	ch'iao
neng	neng	qie	ch'ieh
nong	nung	qin	ch'in
nou	nou	qing	ch'ing
ni	ni	qiong	ch'iung
nian	nien	qiu	ch'iu
niang	niang	qu	ch'ü
niao	niao	quan	ch'üan
nie	nieh	que	ch'üeh
nin	nin	qun	ch'ün
ning	ning	ran	jan
niu	niu	rang	jang
nu	nu	rao	jao
nuan	nuan	re	je
nuo	no	ren	jen
nü	nü	reng	jeng
nüe	nüeh	ri	jih
pa	p'a	rong	jung
pai	p'ai	rou	jou
pan	p'an	ru	ju
pang	p'ang	ruan	juan
pao	p'ao	rui	jui
pei	p'ei	run	jun
pen	p'en	ruo	jo
peng	p'eng	sa	sa
po	p'o	sai	sai
pou	p'ou	san	san
pi	p'i	sang	sang
pian	p'ien	sao	sao
piao	p'iao	se	se
pie	p'ieh	sen	sen
pin	p'in	seng	seng
ping	p'ing	sha	sha
pu	pu	shai	shai
qi	ch'i	shan	shan
qia	ch'ia	shang	shang
qian	ch'ien	shao	shao
qiang	ch'iang	she	she

Pinyin	Wade-Giles	Pinyin	Wade-Giles
shei	shei	tun	t'un
shen	shen	tuo	t'o
sheng	sheng	wa	wa
shi	shih	wai	wai
shou	shou	wan	wan
shu	shu	wang	wang
shua	shua	wei	wei
shuai	shuai	wen	wen
shuan	shuan	weng	weng
shuang	shuang	wo	wo
shui	shui	wu	wu
shun	shun	xi	hsi
shuo	shuo	xia	hsia
si	szu	xian	hsien
song	sung	xiang	hsiang
sou	sou	xiao	hsiao
su	su	xie	hsieh
suan	suan	xin	hsin
sui	sui	xing	hsing
sun	sun	xiong	hsiung
suo	so	xiu	hsiu
ta	t'a	xu	hsü
tai	t'ai	xuan	hsüan
tan	t'an	xue	hsüeh
tang	t'ang	xun	hsün
tao	t'ao	ya	ya
te	t'e	yan	yen
teng	t'eng	yang	yang
ti	t'i	yao	yao
tian	t'ien	ye	yeh
tiao	t'iao	yi	i
tie	t'ieh	yin	yin
ting	t'ing	ying	ying
tong	t'ung	yong	yung
tou	t'ou	you	yu
tu	t'u	yu	yü
tuan	t'uan	yuan	yüan
tui	t'ui	yue	yüeh

Pinyin	Wade-Giles	Pinyin	Wade-Giles
yun	yün	zhi	chih
za	tsa	zhong	chung
zai	tsai	zhou	chou
zan	tsan	zhu	chu
zang	tsang	zhua	chua
zao	tsao	zhuai	chuai
ze	tse	zhuan	chuan
zei	tsei	zhuang	chuang
zen	tsen	zhui	chui
zeng	tseng	zhun	chun
zha	cha	zhuo	cho
zhai	chai	zi	tzu
zhan	chan	zong	tsung
zhang	chang	zou	tsou
zhao	chao	zu	tsu
zhe	che	zuan	tsuan
zhei	chei	zui	tsui
zhen	chen	zun	tsun
zheng	cheng	zuo	tso